UPDATED CHART PATTERN TRADING BOOK

TRADING CHARTS PATTERNS FOR A LIVING: LEARN HOW TO IDENTIFY & TRADE DAILY IN THE FOREX, STOCK MARKETS USING PROFITABLE BEARISH, BULLISH & CONTINUATION CHART PATTERNS.

Trader Dave

Table of Contents

INTRODUCTION

Please allow me to begin by providing a concise introduction to the Bullish Reversal Patterns, Bearish Reversal Patterns, and Continuation Patterns below.

BULLISH REVERSAL PATTERNS

Double Bottom Pattern.

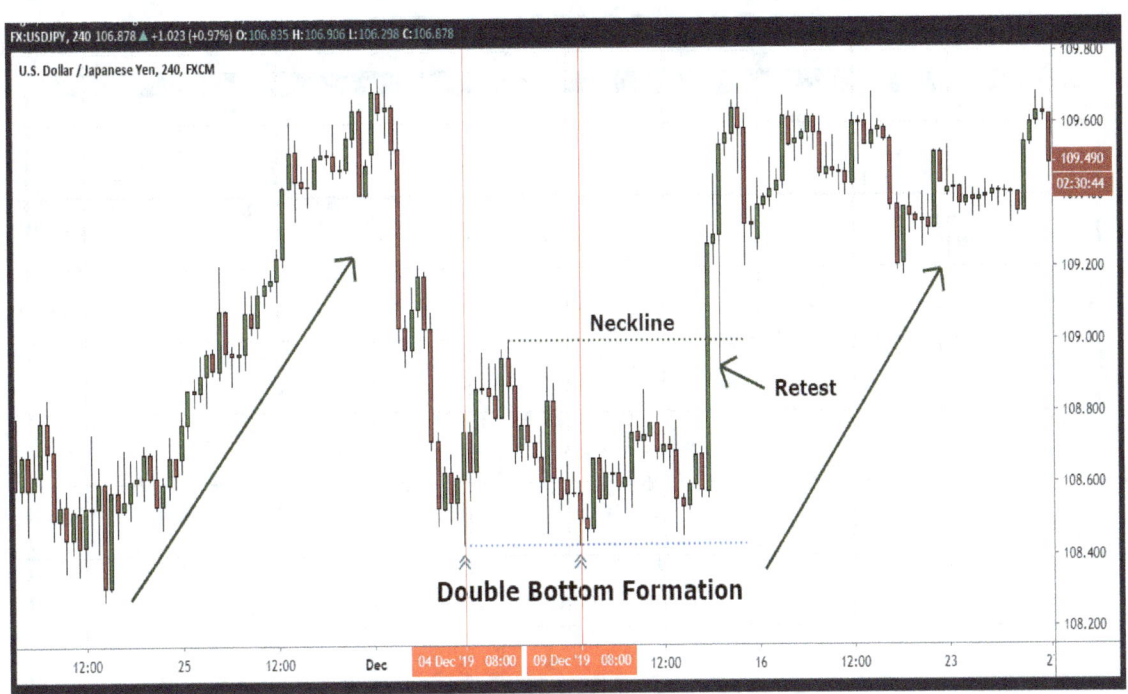

The Double Bottom Pattern is a bullish reversal pattern that signals the potential end of a downtrend and the beginning of an uptrend.

The Double Bottom Pattern usually occurs after an extended downtrend.

It consists of two distinct troughs (bottoms) that form at approximately the same price level. The two bottoms are separated by a peak or a "peak valley," which forms the neckline of the pattern.

The pattern suggests that the downtrend may be exhausting, and a potential reversal to an uptrend is underway. traders look for a confirmation signal when the price breaks above the neckline. The pattern is considered complete when the price breaks decisively above the neckline. This breakout signals a shift in market sentiment from bearish to potentially bullish.

The distance between the lowest point of the pattern and the neckline is measured. This measurement is often used to estimate the potential upward move (target) after the breakout.

TRIPPLE BOTTOM PATTERN

The Triple Bottom Pattern is an extended version of the Double Bottom and is also a bullish reversal pattern. It involves three distinct bottoms occurring consecutively, forming a horizontal line. Similar to the Double Bottom, the pattern is complete with a neckline connecting the peaks between the troughs.

The pattern suggests a more prolonged period of market indecision or selling exhaustion. It reflects a potential reversal from a downtrend to an uptrend. The breakout confirmation occurs when the price decisively breaks above the neckline. This breakout signals a shift in sentiment and a potential reversal to a bullish trend. Just like the Double Bottom, traders often use the distance between the lowest point and the neckline to estimate the potential upward move after the breakout.

FALLING WEDGE (*wedge pattern that falls*.)

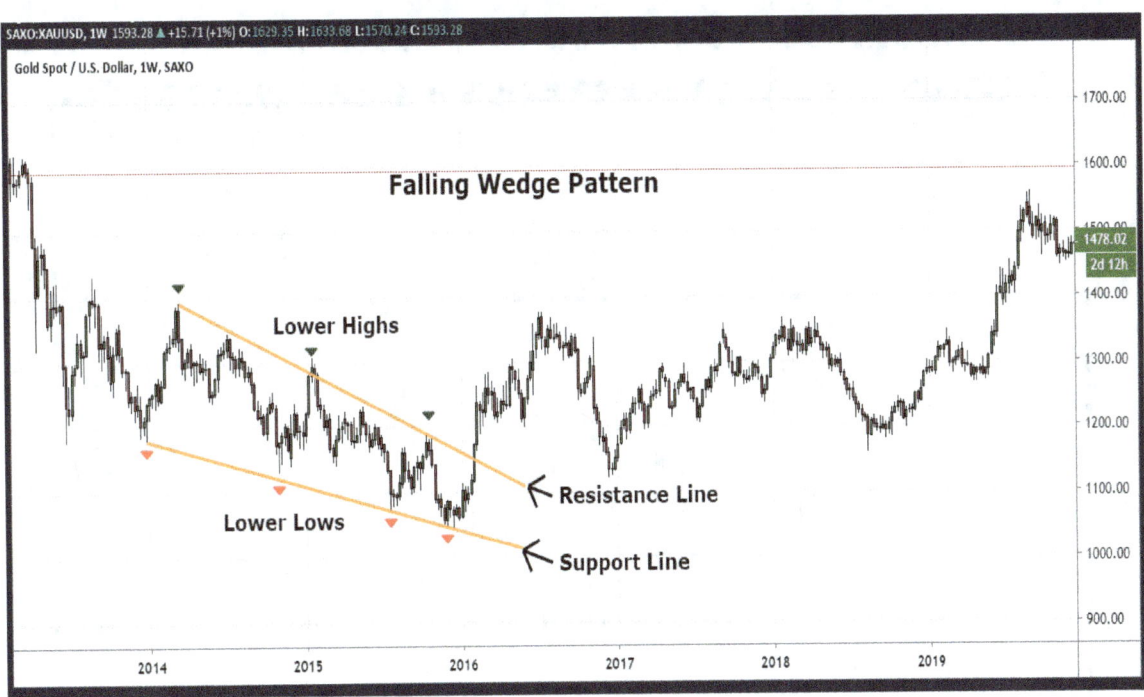

The Falling Wedge is a bullish continuation pattern that typically occurs in a downtrend. It forms when two trendlines converge downward, creating a shape resembling a wedge.

Both trendlines slant in the same direction, indicating a contraction in price volatility. The Falling Wedge is often considered a bullish signal as it suggests a potential reversal of the current downtrend. The converging trendlines imply diminishing selling pressure, and the price may be preparing for an upward breakout.

The pattern is confirmed when the price breaks decisively above the upper trendline. Traders look for increased volume during the breakout to validate the pattern. The target for a Falling Wedge is often estimated by measuring the height of the wedge and projecting it upward from the breakout point.

ROUND BOTTOM PATTERN. (Saucers Bottom)

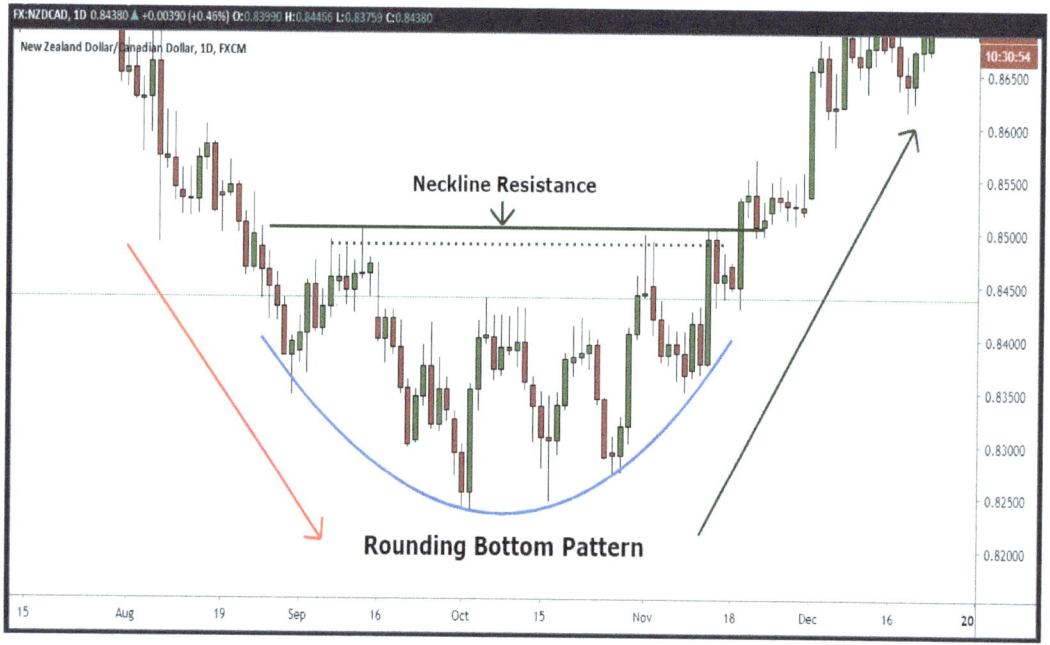

The Round Bottom Pattern is a long-term reversal pattern that indicates a potential shift from a downtrend to an uptrend. It forms a U-shaped or rounded structure over an extended period, resembling the bottom of a saucer. The pattern suggests a gradual transition from bearish sentiment to bullish sentiment in the market. It indicates that selling pressure is waning, and buyers may be gaining control.

The confirmation of the Round Bottom Pattern occurs when the price breaks decisively above the resistance level formed by the saucer's rim. Traders may look for confirmation signals such as increased volume and positive momentum indicators. The target for a Round Bottom is often estimated by measuring the depth of the pattern and projecting it upward from the breakout point.

THE DIAMOND BOTTOM PATTERN.

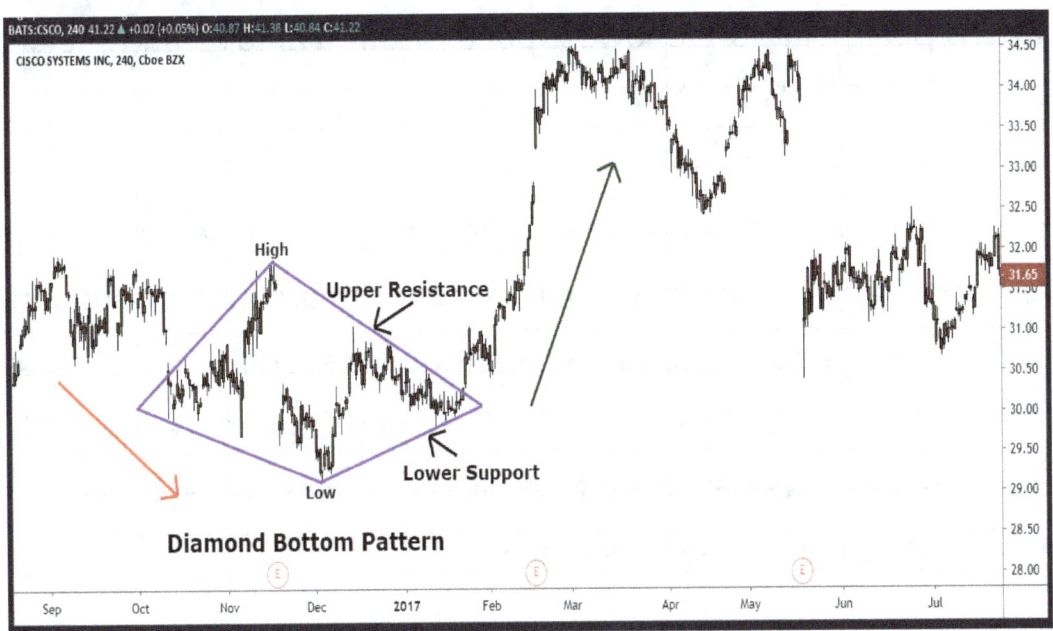

The Diamond Bottom Pattern, also known as the Diamond Reversal Pattern or Diamond Formation, is a rare chart pattern that typically signals a reversal of a downtrend. It is formed by a series of lower highs and higher lows, creating a diamond-shaped pattern on the price chart. The pattern signifies a period of market indecision, with both buyers and sellers struggling for control.

The Diamond Bottom Pattern suggests a transition from a downtrend to a potential uptrend. It indicates that the volatility in the market is decreasing, and a breakout is anticipated. The pattern is often considered a reversal pattern, signaling a shift in sentiment from bearish to bullish.

Confirmation of the Diamond Bottom Pattern occurs when the price breaks decisively above the upper trendline of the diamond. Traders may look for increased volume during the breakout to validate the pattern. The target for a Diamond Bottom Pattern is estimated by measuring the vertical distance from the highest point to the lowest point of the diamond and projecting it upward from the breakout point.

The formation of a Diamond Bottom Pattern may take time, and patience is required for traders awaiting confirmation. Incorporating support and resistance levels into the analysis can provide additional context and confirmation for trading decisions. The Diamond Bottom Pattern reflects a period of market uncertainty and conflicting forces. The breakout often represents a resolution of this uncertainty.

THE V-BOTTOM PATTERN.

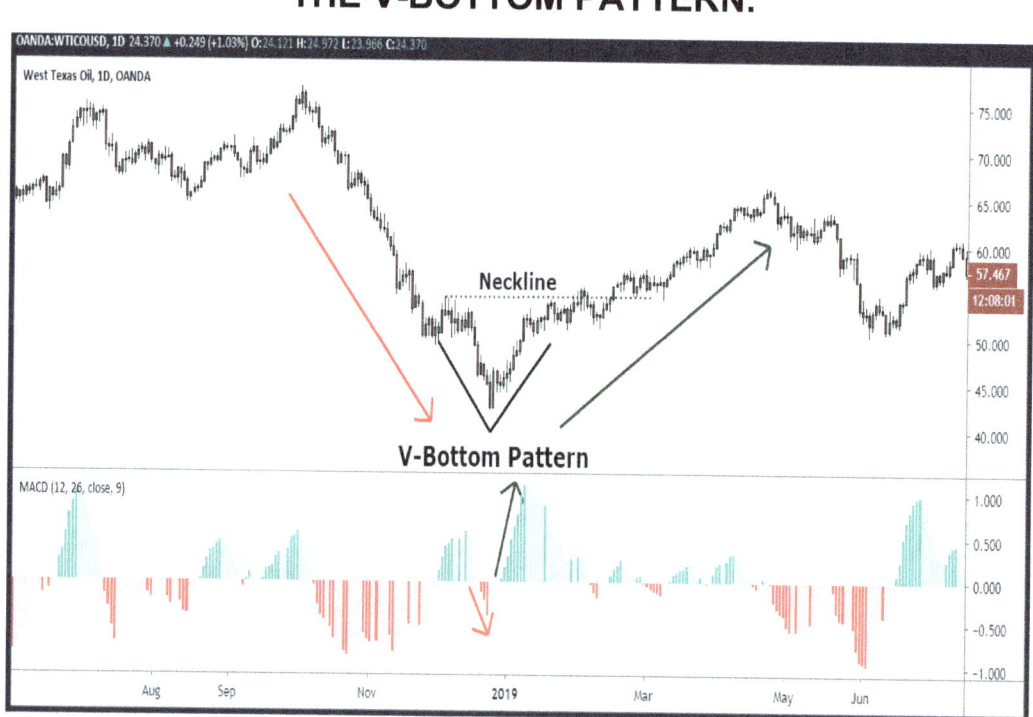

The V-Bottom pattern is a bullish reversal formation characterized by a sharp decline in price, forming a V-shaped bottom. It suggests a swift reversal from a downtrend to an uptrend. This pattern indicates a strong rejection of lower prices and a potential shift in market sentiment from bearish to bullish. Traders often look for confirmation through increased buying volume.

BEARISH REVERSAL PATTERNS.

The DOUBLE TOP PATTERNS (pattern with double tops).

The Double Top pattern is a bearish reversal pattern with two peaks at almost the same price level, separated by a trough (neckline). It signifies a potential end to an uptrend. Traders typically consider the Double Top pattern complete when the price breaks and closes below the neckline. This breach suggests a shift from bullish to bearish market conditions.

TRIPLE-TOP PATTERN.

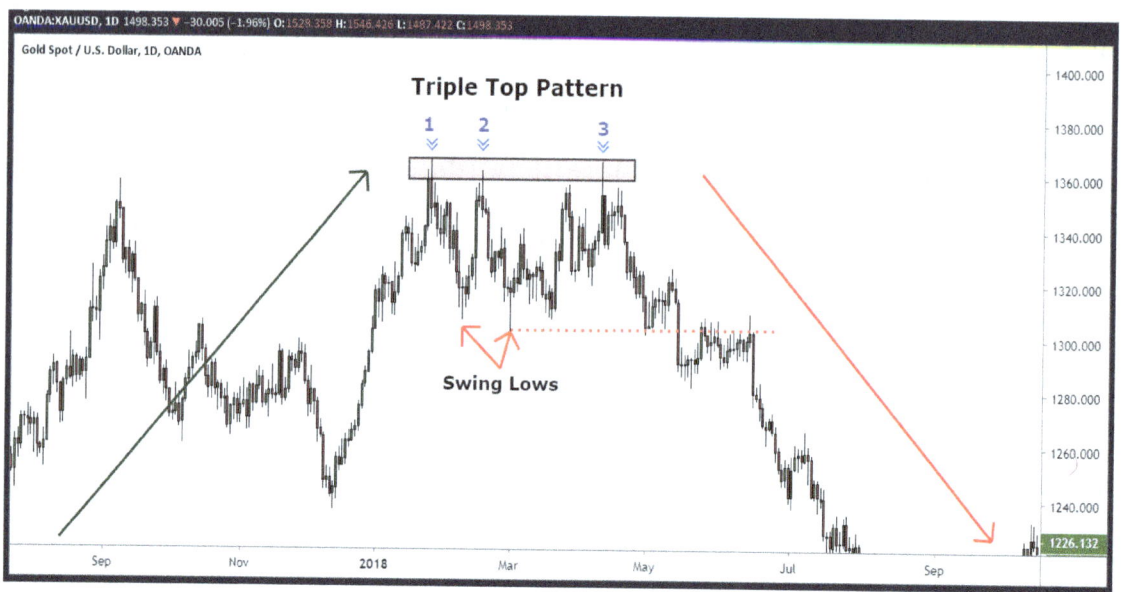

Similar to the Double Top, the Triple Top pattern is a bearish reversal pattern that involves three peaks at approximately the same level. It signals a potential weakening of an existing uptrend. Traders watch for confirmation by observing a break below the neckline. This breach indicates increased selling pressure and a potential trend reversal

THE RISING WEDGE PATTERN.

The Rising Wedge is a bearish reversal pattern formed by two ascending trendlines that converge. It suggests a potential trend reversal from bullish to bearish. As the price breaks through the lower support line, it confirms the completion of the pattern and may indicate a shift in market sentiment. Traders often look for additional signals like increased volume to validate the reversal.

THE ROUNDING TOP PATTERN

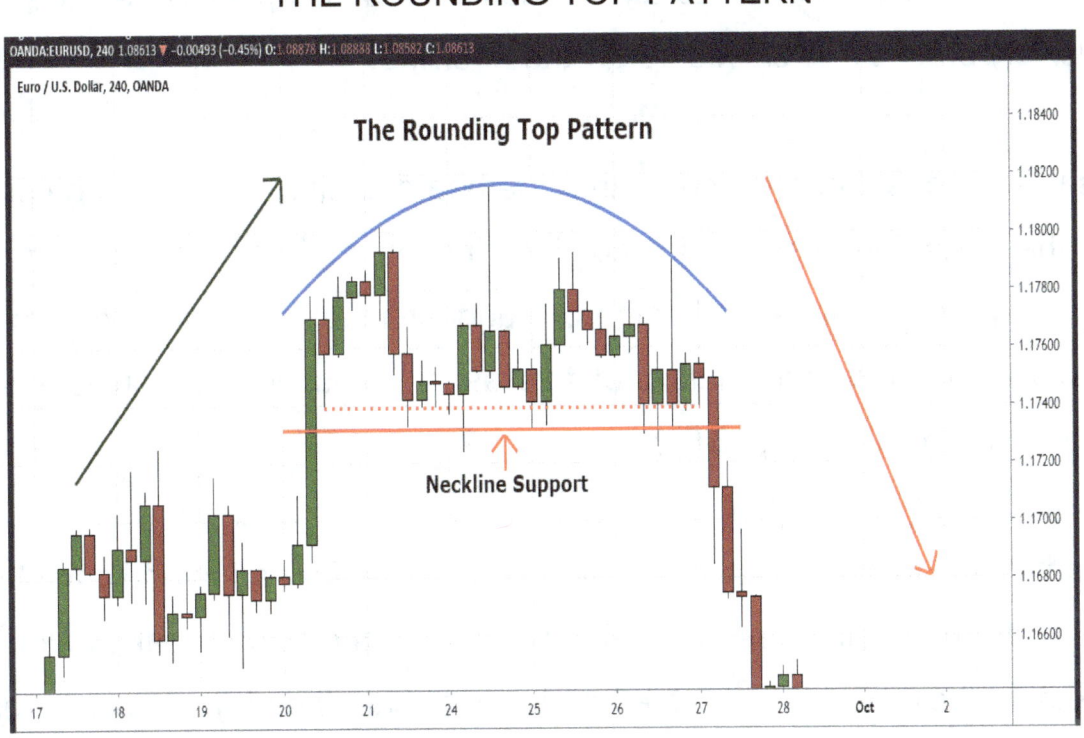

The Rounding Top chart pattern is a significant technical formation in financial markets, particularly in the context of technical analysis for trading. This pattern is identified by a distinctive curved or rounded shape, resembling the upper part of a circle or an arch, formed by the price action on a price chart. It is also known as a "saucer top" due to its appearance.

The Rounding Top typically occurs after a prolonged uptrend in the market. It signals a potential reversal of the existing upward trend. This pattern is accompanied by a neckline support, which is a horizontal line connecting the lows between the rounded tops. This neckline represents a critical level of support that the price has repeatedly failed to break through during the formation of the pattern.

During the formation of the Rounding Top, the price gradually rises, creating the rounded shape. This suggests a loss of momentum and a potential shift in market sentiment. The pattern is considered complete when the price decisively breaks and closes below the neckline.

This breach of support indicates that the bears (sellers) are gaining control, and the bulls (buyers) are losing their influence. The completion of the Rounding Top is a bearish signal, suggesting that a trend reversal is underway. Traders often interpret this as an indication to consider short positions or to exit long positions.

It is advisable to analyze trading volume during the formation and completion of the pattern. An increase in selling volume as the price breaks below the neckline adds confirmation to the bearish reversal. The projected price target for the downside move is often estimated by measuring the distance from the highest point of the rounding top to the neckline and extending that distance downward from the breakout point.

THE DIAMOND TOP PATTERN.:

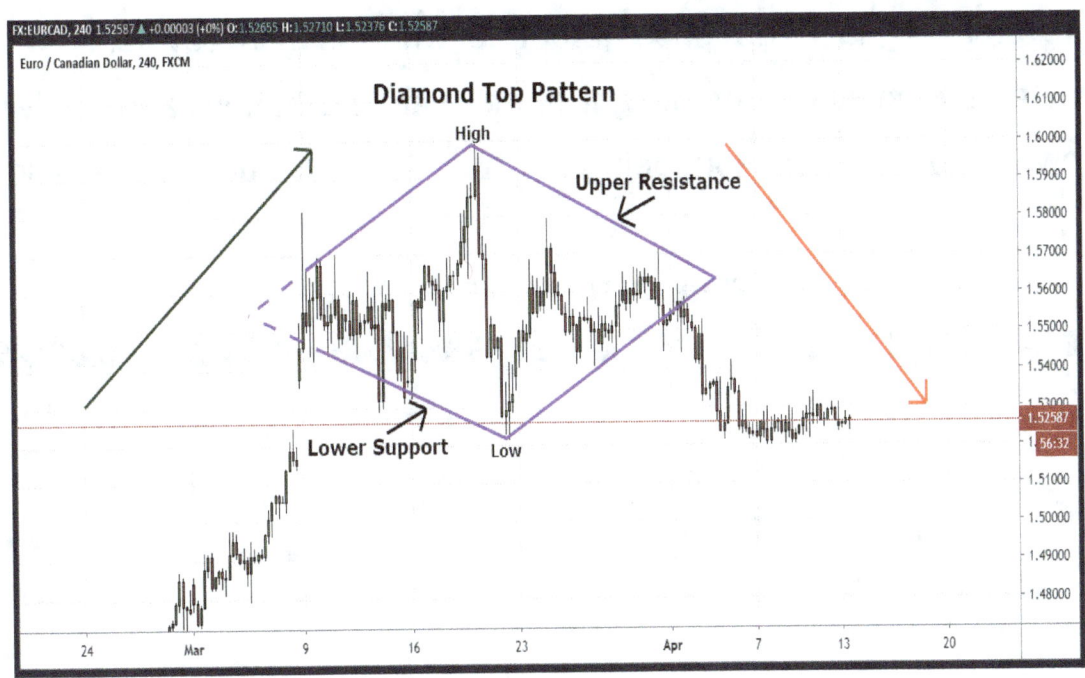

The Diamond Top Pattern is a technical chart formation that occurs during an uptrend and signals a potential reversal in the market. It gets its name from the diamond shape it creates on the price chart. The Diamond Top forms after a sustained uptrend and is characterized by two converging trendlines, one representing higher highs and the other representing lower highs. This creates a diamond shape on the chart.

This pattern typically takes some time to develop, as it reflects a period of indecision and a struggle between buyers and sellers. The breakout from a Diamond Top is usually in the opposite direction of the preceding trend. If the price breaks below the lower trendline, it signals a bearish reversal, and if it breaks above the upper trendline, it indicates a bullish continuation.

Traders often analyze volume during the formation of the pattern. An increase in volume during the breakout adds confirmation to the validity of the reversal signal. The price target for the bearish reversal is often estimated by measuring the height of the diamond pattern and applying it downward from the breakout point. For a bullish continuation, the height is measured upward.

THE V TOP PATTERN.

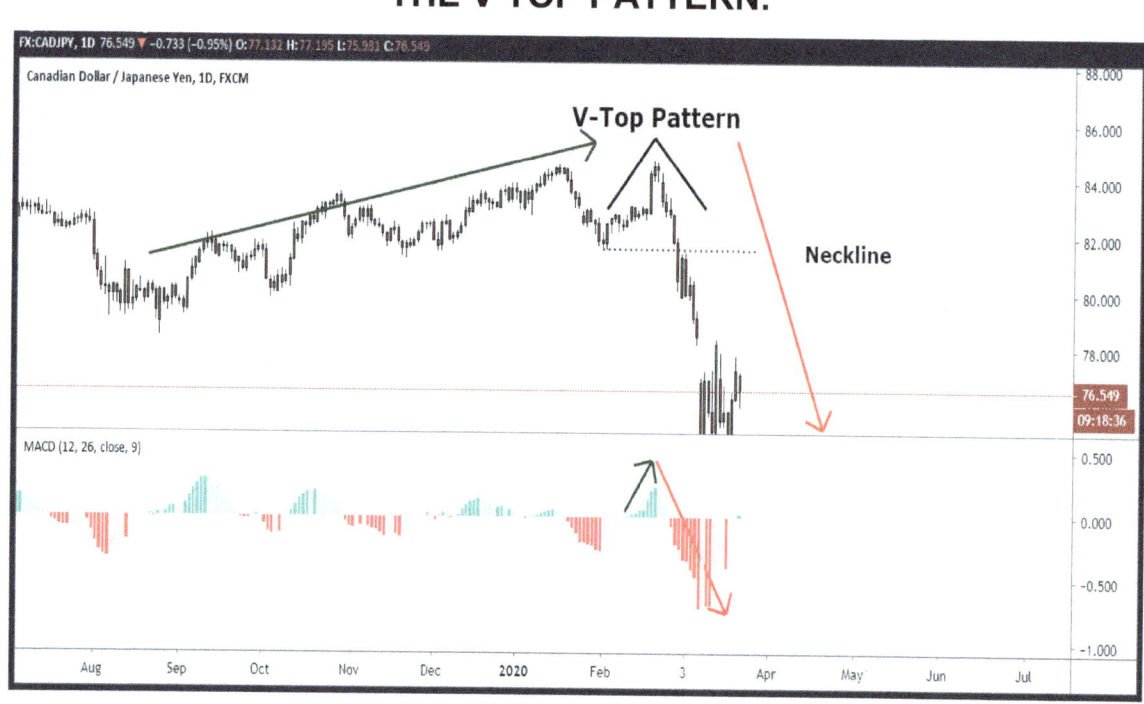

The V Top Pattern is a bearish reversal pattern that resembles the letter "V" on a price chart. It signifies a potential change in trend direction from bullish to bearish.

The V Top forms after a significant uptrend when the price makes a sharp upward move, creating a V-shaped peak. It indicates that buyers have pushed the price to an extreme level, and a reversal is likely. Unlike some other reversal patterns that take time to develop, the V Top suggests a rapid shift in market sentiment. The sharp upward move is followed by an equally swift decline. Volume analysis is crucial in confirming the pattern. An increase in selling volume during the downward move provides additional support for the bearish reversal.

The confirmation of the V Top occurs when the price breaks below the low point of the V. This breach indicates that sellers have taken control. Traders often estimate a price target for the downside move by measuring the height of the V and projecting it downward from the breakdown point.

THE TRIANGLE PETTERN.

The Triangle Pattern is a technical chart pattern that forms when the price movement of an asset creates a triangular shape on a price chart. This pattern indicates a period of consolidation and tightening volatility, suggesting an impending breakout. There are three main types of triangles: Symmetrical Triangle: Two converging trendlines, one representing higher lows and the other lower highs, form a symmetrical triangle. The breakout can be either to the upside or downside. It typically occurs around two-thirds of the way through the pattern.

Ascending Triangle: A horizontal resistance line and an ascending trendline create an ascending triangle. The breakout is usually to the upside, signaling a continuation of the existing uptrend.

Descending Triangle: A horizontal support line and a descending trendline create a descending triangle. The breakout is typically to the downside, signaling a continuation of the existing downtrend.

THE FLAG AND PENNANT.

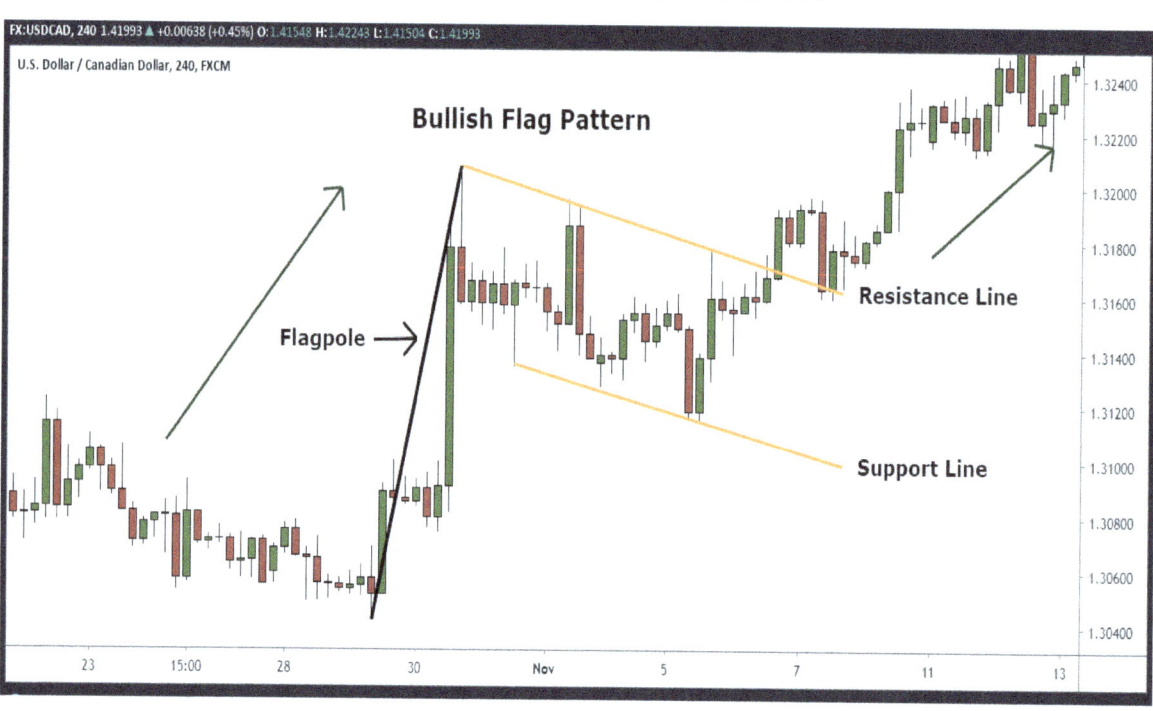

The Flag and Pennant Patterns are short-term continuation patterns that signal a brief consolidation before the previous trend resumes. The flag pattern resembles a rectangular-shaped flag on the chart, with parallel trendlines. Flags are typically short-term and form after a strong price movement. The breakout occurs in the same direction as the preceding trend. The pennant pattern is similar to a symmetrical triangle, forming after a strong price movement. Pennants are also short-term patterns. Like flags, pennants lead to breakouts in the direction of the preceding trend.

THE CUP AND HANDLE PATTERN.

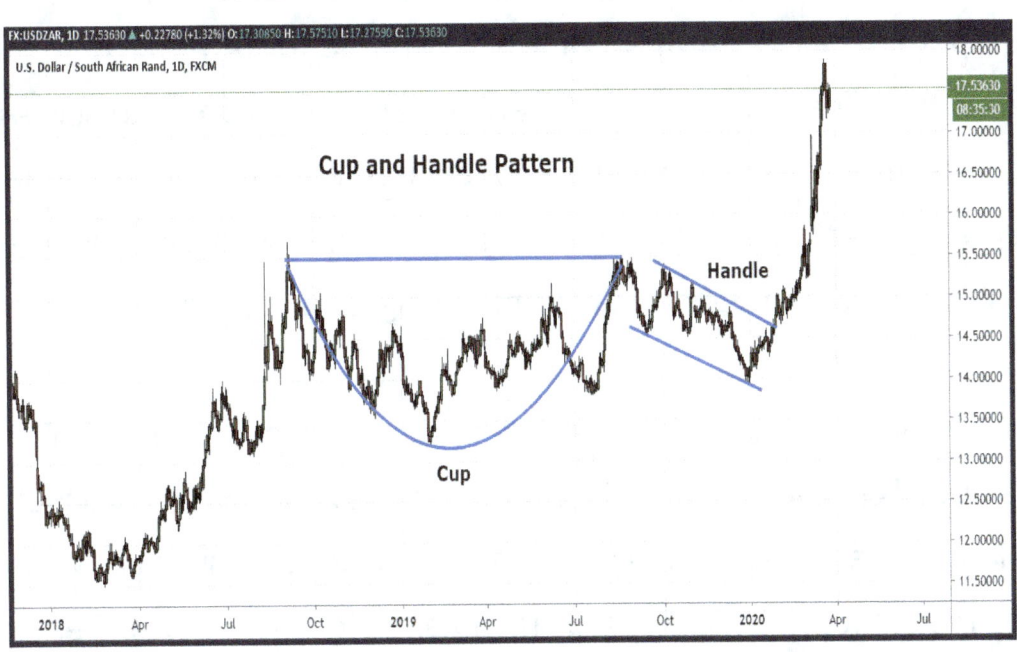

The Cup and Handle Pattern is a bullish continuation pattern that resembles the shape of a tea cup on a price chart. It consists of two parts: The cup and handle formation. The left side of the cup involves a gradual rounding bottom, followed by a steeper rise forming the right side. The cup formation may take several weeks to months to develop.

After the cup, a consolidation or retracement forms the handle, typically a smaller downward-sloping price movement. The handle is relatively shorter in duration. The breakout occurs when the price moves upward from the handle, indicating a continuation of the bullish trend.

Best Chart Patterns

There is no single "best" chart pattern because they are all employed to draw attention to various trends across a wide range of markets. In candlestick trading, chart patterns are frequently used, which slightly simplifies the process of seeing previous market opens and closes. In a volatile market, some patterns work better than others. Some patterns work best in bullish markets, while others work best in bearish markets. In light of this, it is crucial to understand the "best" chart pattern to use for your specific market, as using the incorrect one or being unsure of which one to use could result in you missing out on an opportunity to make significant profit.

It is crucial that I briefly explain support and resistance levels before delving into the specifics of various chart patterns. The level at which an asset's price stops declining and begins to rise again is referred to as support. When price reaches resistance, it typically stops rising and dips back down. Demand and supply, or the balance between buyers and sellers, determines the levels of support and resistance that develop. A market's price will typically increase when there are more buyers than sellers (or when there is a greater demand than there is supply). When there are more sellers than buyers, the price typically decreases (more supply than demand).

For instance, if demand is greater than supply, the price of an asset may be increasing. The price will eventually rise to the level at which consumers are prepared to part with their money, and at that point, demand will decline. The decision to close one's positions by buyers may occur at this point.

As more and more buyers close their positions, this creates resistance, and the price begins to decline toward a level of support as supply starts to outpace demand. A level of support is reached where supply and demand start to balance out once the price of an asset has sufficiently decreased. At this point, buyers may choose to reenter the market because the asset is now more affordable. As demand starts to rise relative to supply, it will push the price back up toward a level of resistance if the increased buying persists. A level of resistance might change to a level of support once a price pass through it.

What Makes Chart Patterns Important.

In trade, chart patterns are important because they have a lot to do with how people think about price movement. Price chart analysis has been around since the 1600s.

Japanese candlestick charts give you more information, like the high and low points of an asset's price shift. This makes it easier to look at how prices change over time. It's important not to mix up price pattern analysis with candlestick chart pattern analysis, which looks at whether one candle is bearish or bullish.

Most of the time, candlestick patterns repeat the movement, making price patterns that look like numbers. These candlestick patterns can help both experienced and new traders guess how prices will move in the future and place winning trades, setting clear profit targets for that movement.

Price candlestick charts exhibit several stock chart patterns, including double bottom, double top, head and shoulders, inverted head and shoulders, rising wedges, falling wedges, flag, ascending triangle, descending triangle, and more.

Traders need to use chart trends to look at how the market is moving and make smart choices. These patterns help traders spot possible trends and reversals and give them clues about how people in the market are feeling.

Head and Shoulders pattern

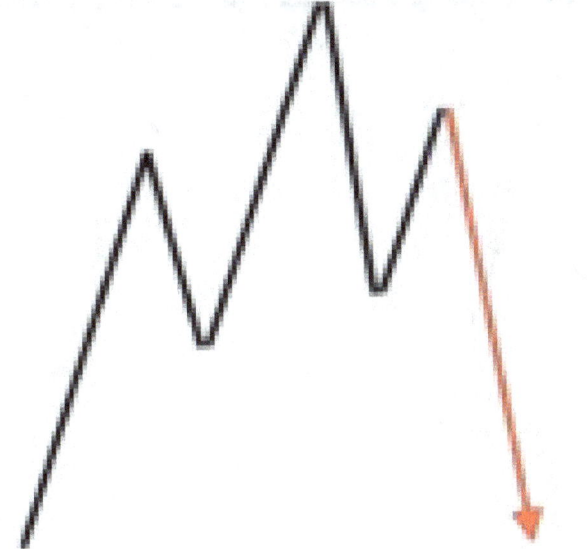

Inverse Head and Shoulders pattern

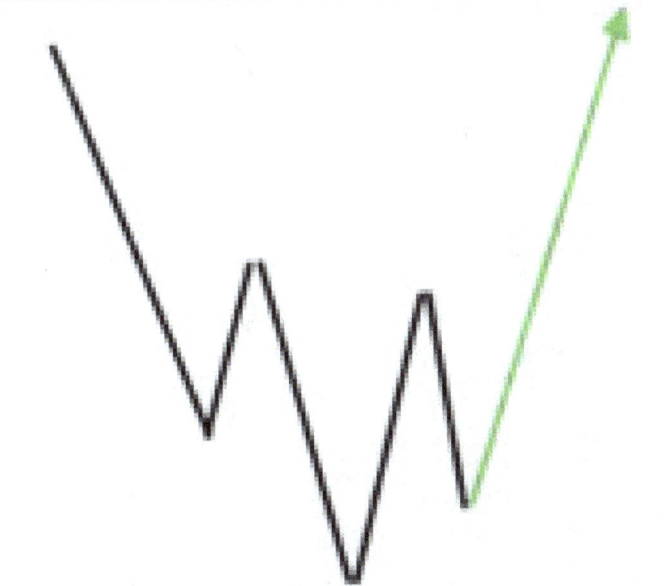

23

Double Bottom pattern

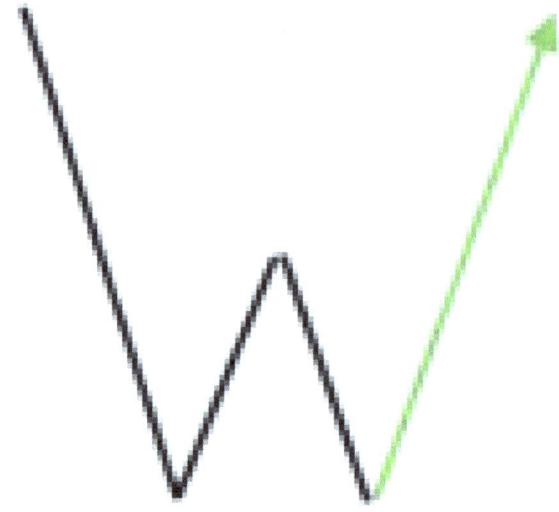

Double Top pattern

Bullish and Bearish Flag patterns

Rising Wedge in an uptrend

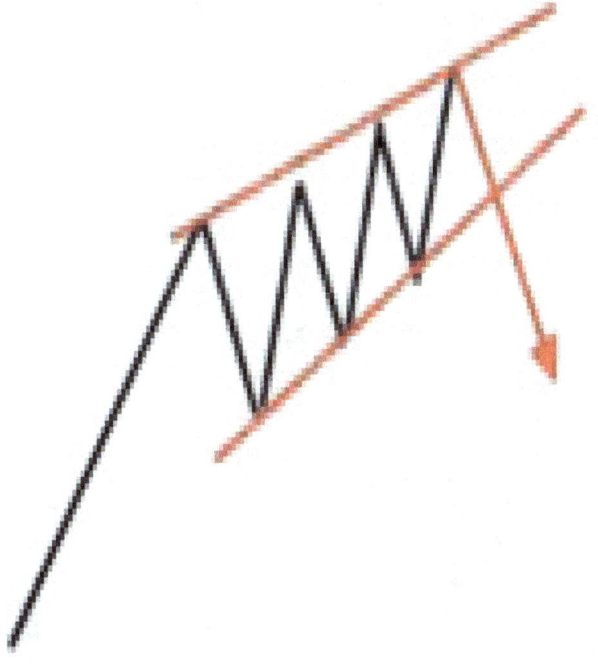

Falling Wedge
in an uptrend

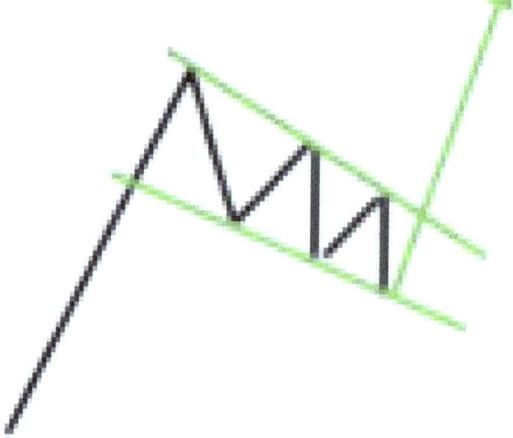

Rising Wedge
in a downtrend

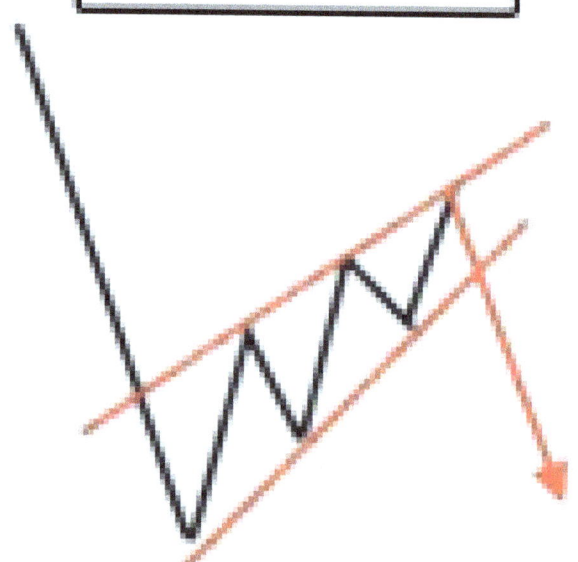

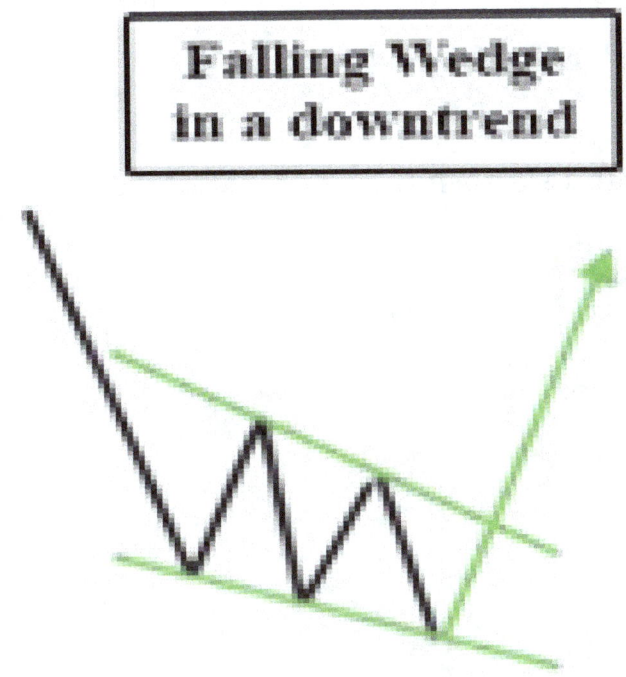

How to Read Patterns on a Forex Chart

Day traders use Forex chart patterns to figure out the way of price changes by looking at how prices have moved in the past. The main job of graphic chart patterns is to give traders the information they need to decide whether to go short or long. The trader's goal is to make money by using statistical and graphics data to make deals. With the help of Japanese patterns, bars, and lines, it's easy to spot trends on chats. In chart analysis, there are two kinds of candlestick patterns:

1. **Bearish and Bullish Reversal Patterns**
- Head and shoulders
- Head and shoulders turned upside down;

- Double bottom

- Double top

- Rising wedge in an uptrend

2. Trend continuation Patterns:

- Rising wedge in a downtrend

- Falling wedge in an upward trend

- Bullish trend rectangle

- Bearish trend rectangle

- Bullish pennant

- Bearish Pennant

- Symmetrical Triangle

- Ascending triangle

- Descending triangle

The Cup and handle pattern

The Cup and Handle Pattern is a bullish continuation pattern that resembles the shape of a tea cup on a price chart. It consists of two parts: The cup and handle formation. The left side of the cup involves a gradual rounding bottom, followed by a steeper rise forming the right side. The cup formation may take several weeks to months to develop.

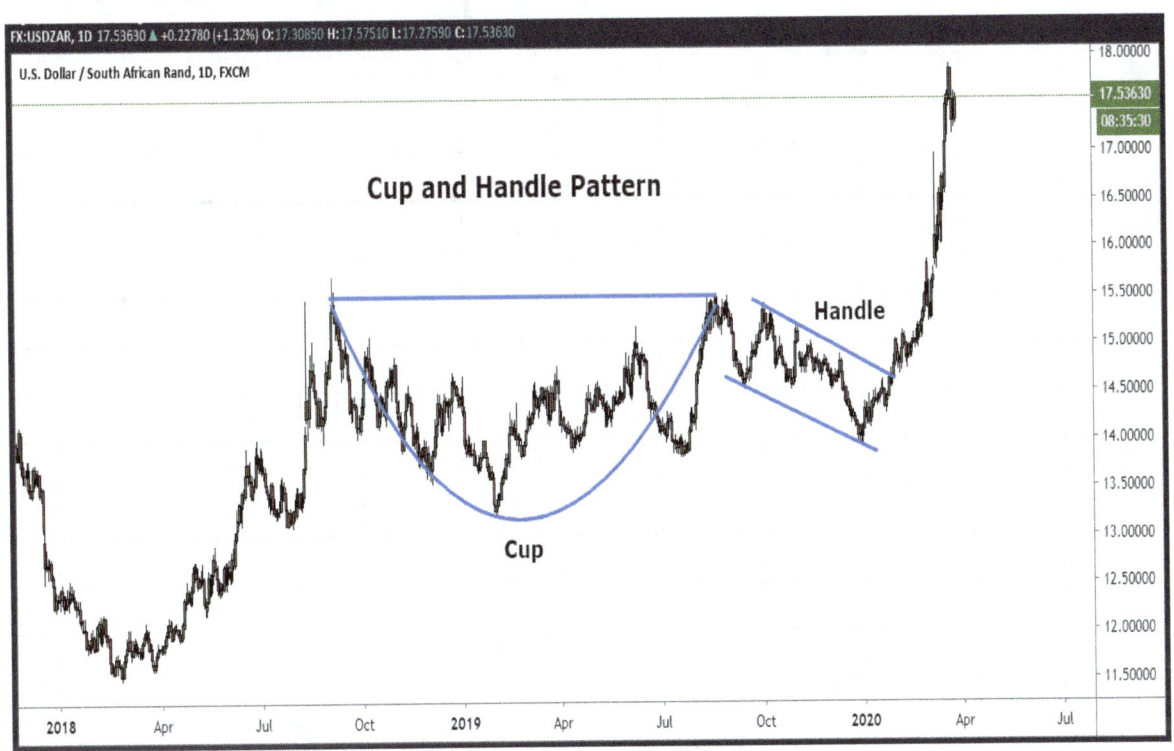

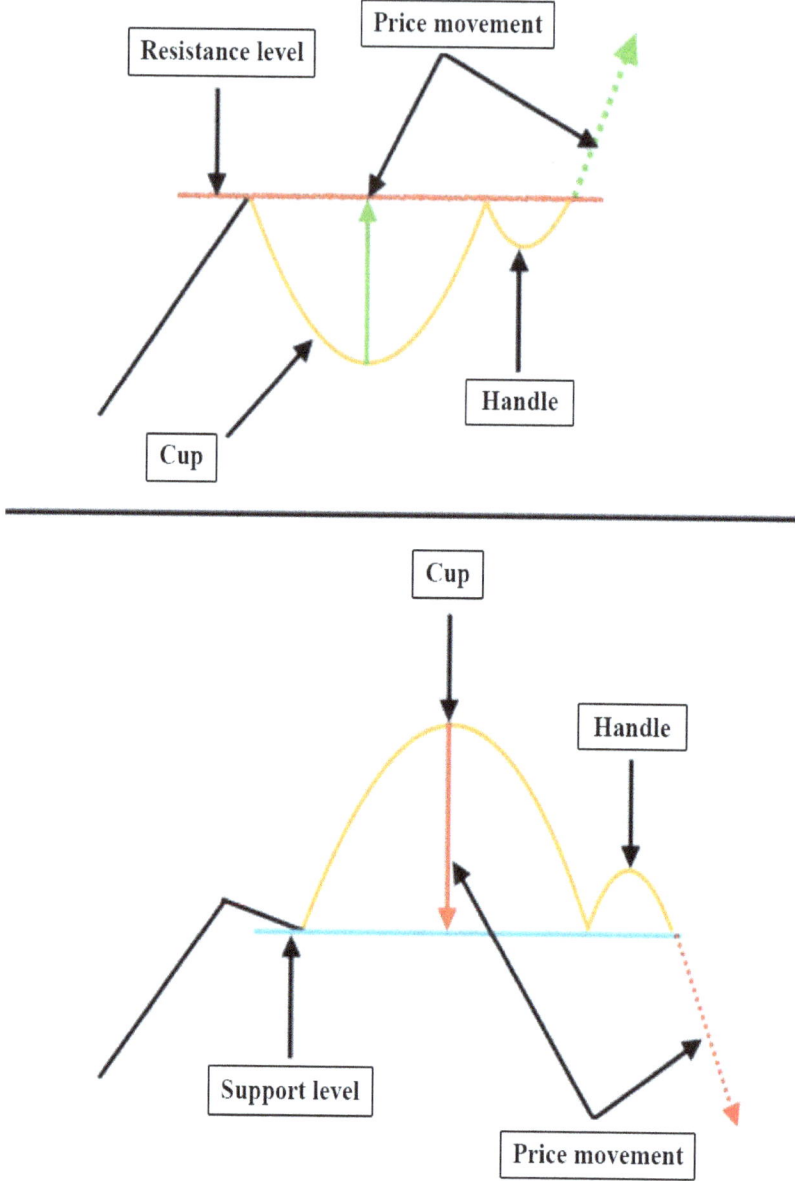

You can see an example of a cup and handle pattern on this fifteen-minute EURUSD chart. You could open a trade after the pattern was fully formed and the broken resistance level was retested. The picture shows that the resistance level turned into a support level and a bearish hammer candlestick pattern formed above it. Getting out of the handle was a signal to go long.

The price movement is determined by measuring the distance from the lowest point of the cup to the level of resistance or beyond. Position the stop loss below the recently established support line.

The USD/ZAR pair went through a cup and handle pattern that started in late 2019 and finished in early 2020. You can see it in the chart above. After that, the price broke out of the pattern and began going back up.

The handle part of the overall pattern is often marked by trendlines and moves lower after a corrective structure that, ideally, doesn't go back too far into the cup. Once price leaves the handle's consolidation or correction phase, the cup and handle pattern are said to be over.

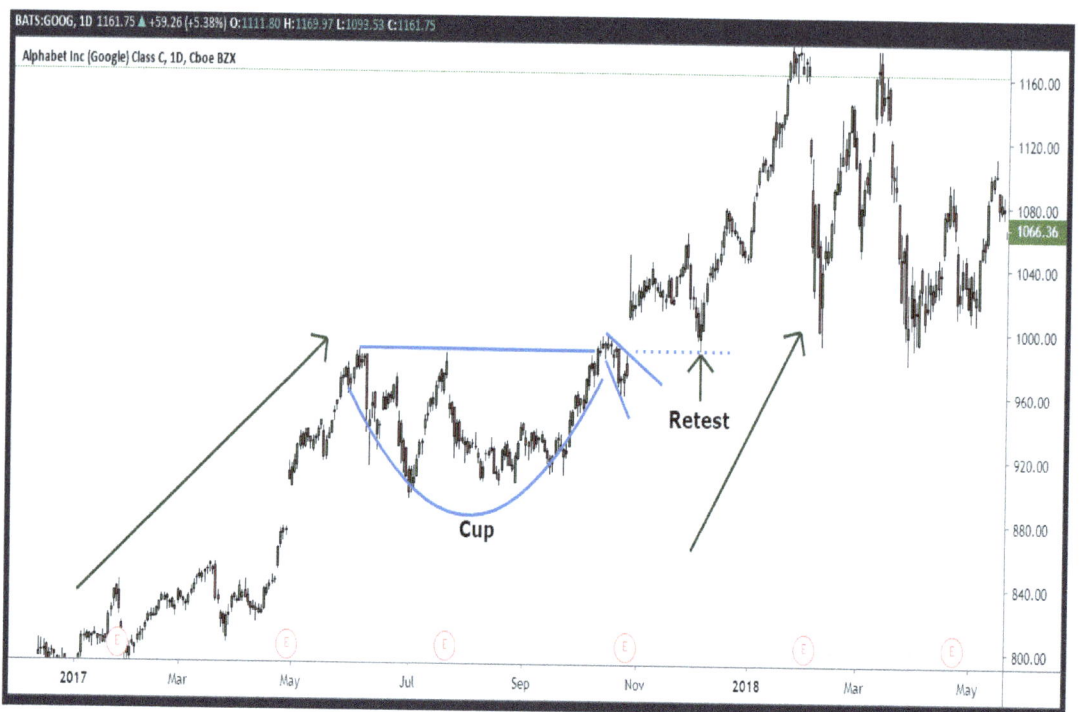

A second cup-and-handle pattern was seen in Google chart during the middle of 2017. Not every cup and handle Pattern will be perfect. In this case, the handle started to form just above the horizontal part of the cup.

When the pattern was over, the price spiked above the cup, but it later fell back and tried the top of the teacup again, giving traders another chance to buy Google stock.

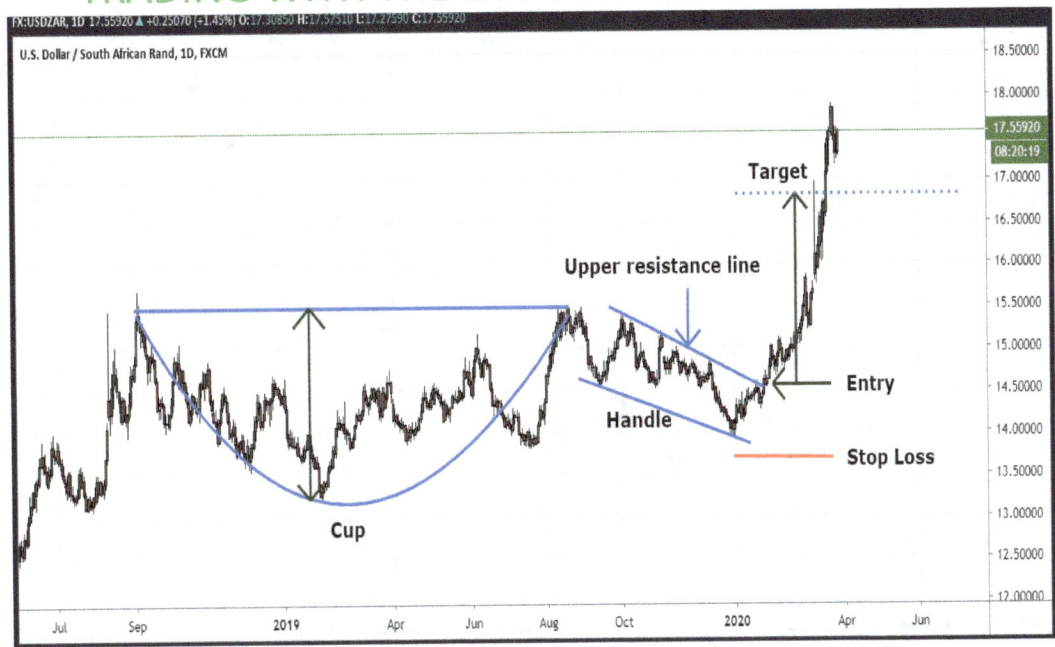

Since this is a continuation pattern that favors the bull, aggressive traders will often place a buy order as soon as the price crosses above the upper resistance line of the handle. On the other hand, conservative traders will usually wait for the price to cross the upper line and only enter if it retests the resistance line.

But sometimes, the next move up could be so strong that price won't even try to test the support line again, leaving traders without the chance to buy. One can find a profit target by measuring the distance from the cup's lowest point and adding that distance to the breaking level.

Once you have opened a long trade, you can set a stop loss below the lowest point of the handle if the possible reward is higher than the risk.

The last chart shows how a long investment would have grown in the Google case we used earlier. After reporting earnings, Google's stock price spiked above the upper resistance line of the handle.

However, the price did return to the breakout point, which made it a great time to buy. One of the easiest trade patterns to spot on a chart is the cup and handle pattern, which has clear rules for where to place your entry, stop loss, and target. It's an accurate strong technical sign that the trend will continue to go up.

THE TRIANGLES PATTERNS

Triangle patterns on the chart make it hard to guess how prices will move because there are three different kinds of these patterns.

ADVANTAGES OF THE TRIANGLE PATTERN IN TRADING

Utilizing this pattern has the clear benefit that when it works, you will usually observe a sharp break.

This is because there has been a steady rise in either buying or selling volume. As a result, bears or bulls trying to protect the support or resistance level will usually have to give up their positions. Most of the time, stops are put just above the levels. When they are taken away, more people sell or buy.

DISADVANTAGES OF THE TRIANGLE PATTERN IN TRADING

An issue with the triangle pattern is that it can lead to false breaks.

This is also true for the triangle pattern, even though I've talked about it before in relation to other strategies. I have, however, used this approach before, and while there are false breaks, they happen much less often than with other trading methods I've talked about in this book.

Even though no method is 100 percent foolproof, I am sure that this one can work well without any extra signs, at least to a large degree.

As always, you must back test any strategy you intend to use rigorously on the asset you are trading because sometimes, particular strategies simply perform better on particular assets.

The Symmetrical Triangle

This kind of continuation pattern forms when price swing highs and lows get smaller. Right now, it's hard to tell how the quotes will move because there is a big chance of falling into bearish or bullish traps that can cause you to lose money quickly. That's why it's important to wait for the triangle to be confirmed up or down and the price to consolidate higher. It's also a good idea to wait until the price tests the broken level.

When prices change, quotes either go up or down in a way that is equal to the price change.

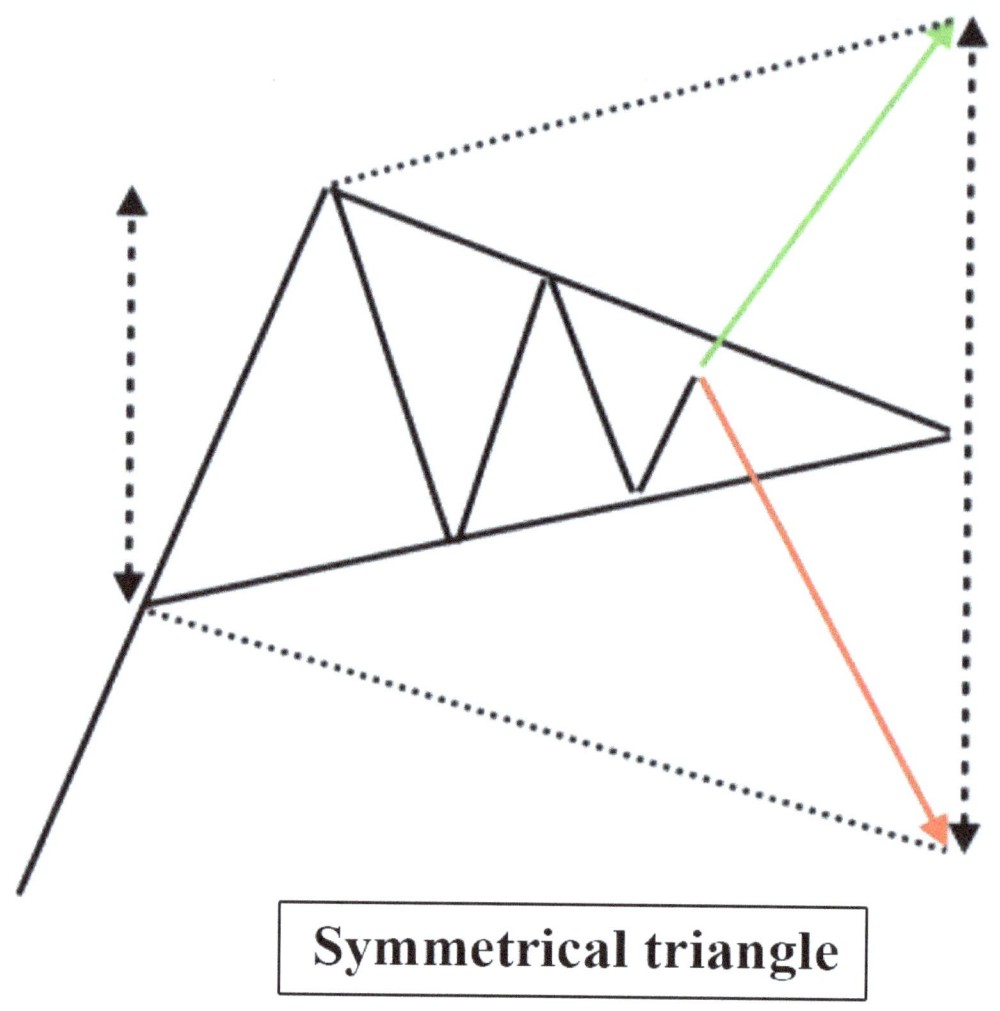

Symmetrical triangle

On the 30-minute UKBRENT price chart, there is a symmetrical triangle. You can see that both bulls and bears tried to get caught. Right now, you should wait for the triangle to break up or down before making a decision. Your stop loss should be in the middle of the narrowing channel. To get a more accurate picture, you should use Japanese candlestick patterns analysis.

The bears tried to break through the bottom edge of the triangle, but the bulls pushed back, setting up a candle squeeze trap for the bears.

You should wait for the price to finally consolidate before making a trade in this case.

Ascending Triangle

There is a clear horizontal resistance line in the ascending triangle which is a continuation pattern. When the quotes reach it, they turn around and made rising lows. After some consolidation, the price of the asset breaks through this level of resistance, and it keeps going up until it reaches the height of the ascending triangle.

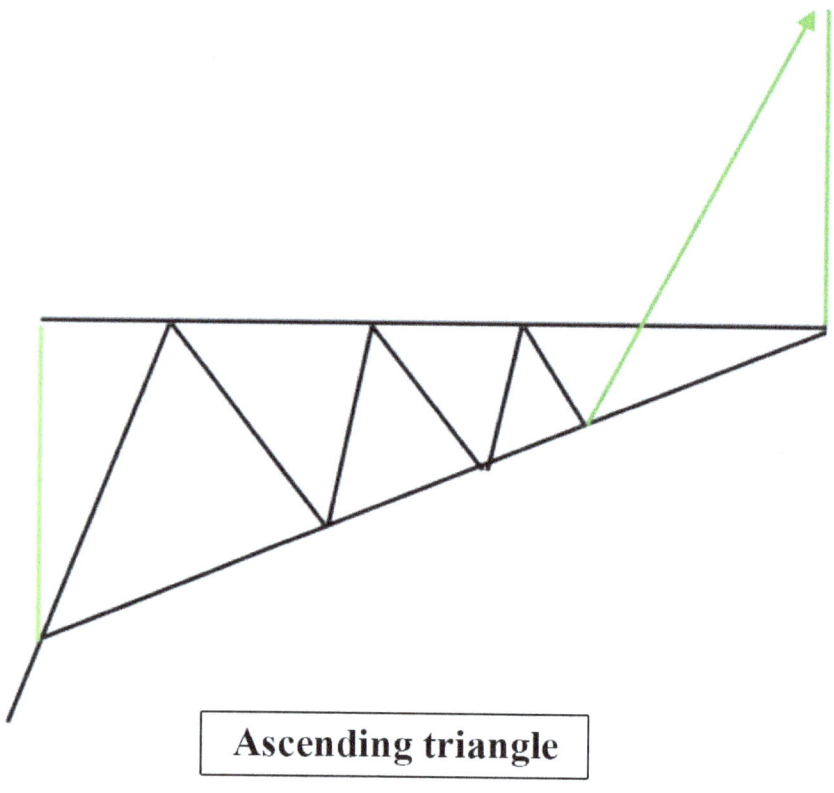

Ascending triangle

On this 30-minute BTCUSD picture, you can see how a rising triangle forms. As you can see in the chart below, a resistance level formed along with rising lows. There was then an impulse breakout of quotes and price consolidation above the resistance. After testing the level again, there was a chance to open a buy position with the target at the top of the triangle. In this case, the stop loss is set below the broken resistance line, which is equal to the distance of the low of the impulse candle.

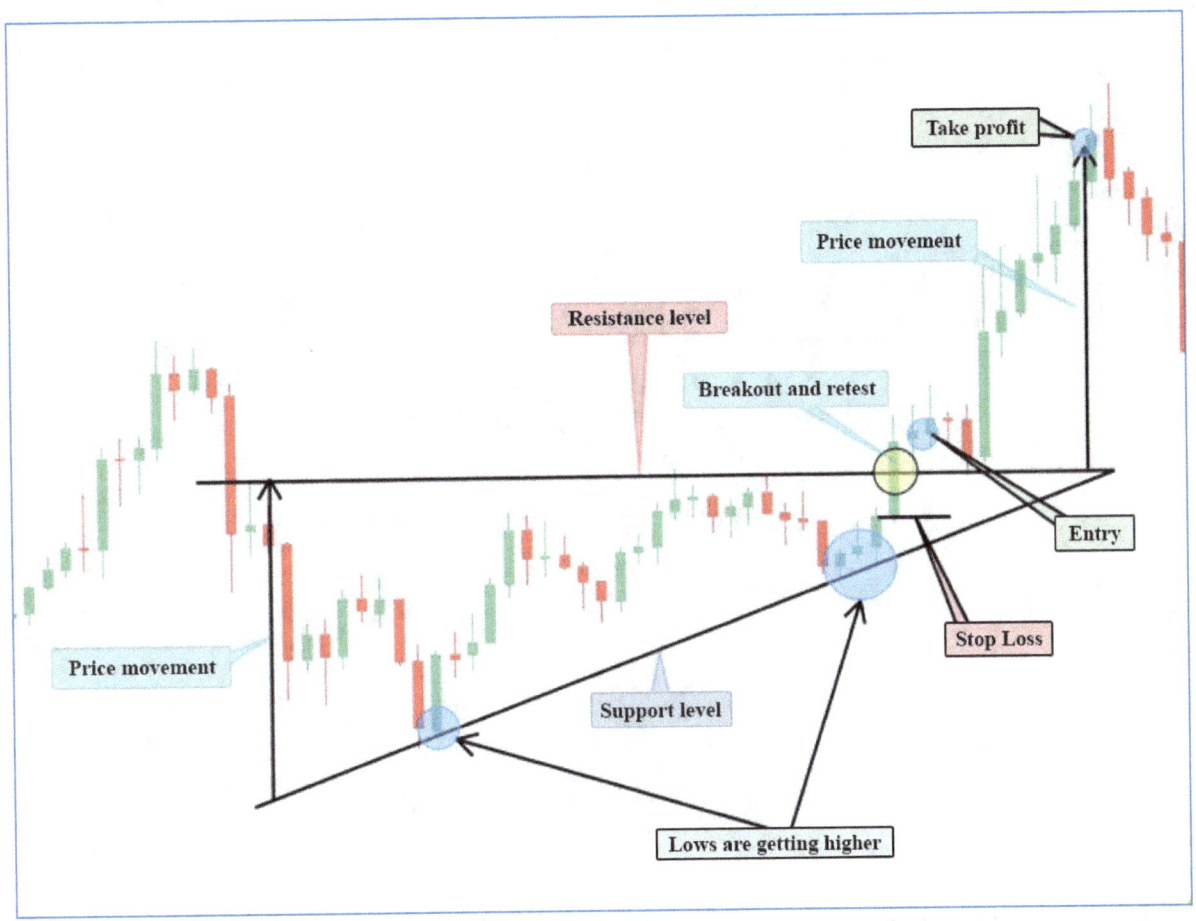

Descending Triangle

That is not the same as the rising triangle continuation pattern. In this case, there is a clear support level and a smooth drop in highs. This breaks the lower price trend line, and the price keeps falling quickly until it reaches the height of the triangle.

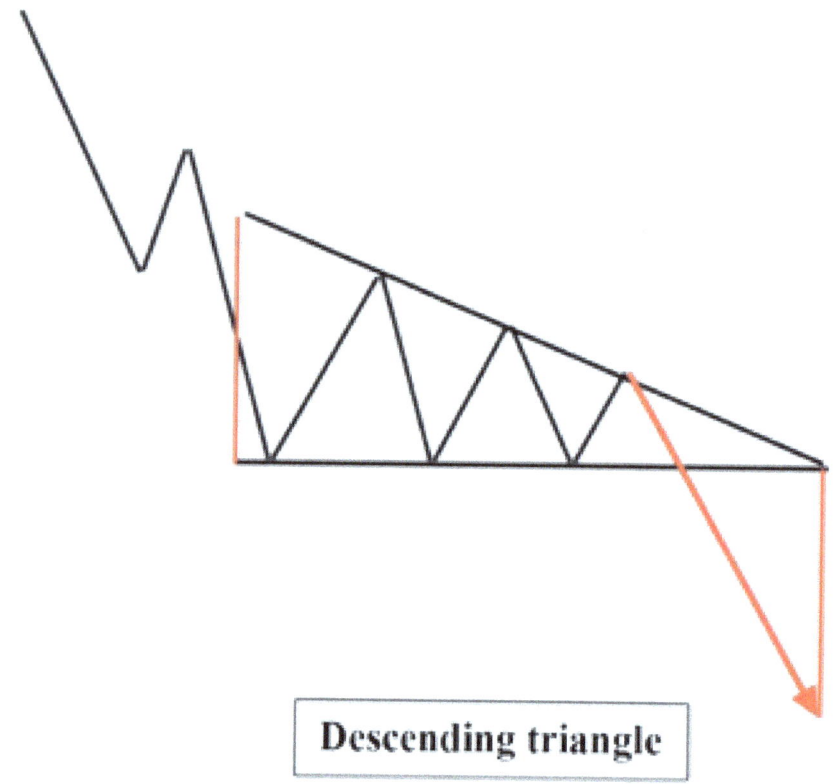

Descending triangle

You can see the descending triangle on the 15-minute chart of the XAUUSD below. The formation of the candlestick pattern is also easy to see. Quotes were stopped from moving below the support level several times, and the instrument's highs are going down. After the asset's price went down, the support level was broken. A short sale can only be made after the price goes down and stays below the support line.

To determine the take profit level, it is advisable to calculate the vertical distance of the triangle, similar to other variations of this candlestick formation. The stop loss in this scenario is positioned above the support level.

The Flag Pattern

The flag is a pattern that indicates the continuation of a trend. There are two distinct types: **The Bullish Flag And The Bearish Flag.** The price establishes a flagpole, followed by the placement of the flag and a breakdown of quotations when the price moves beyond the flag, determined by the height of the flagpole.

This candlestick pattern is ideal for intraday trading on timescales of 5, 15, or 30 minutes and is considered one of the most effective patterns for day trading.

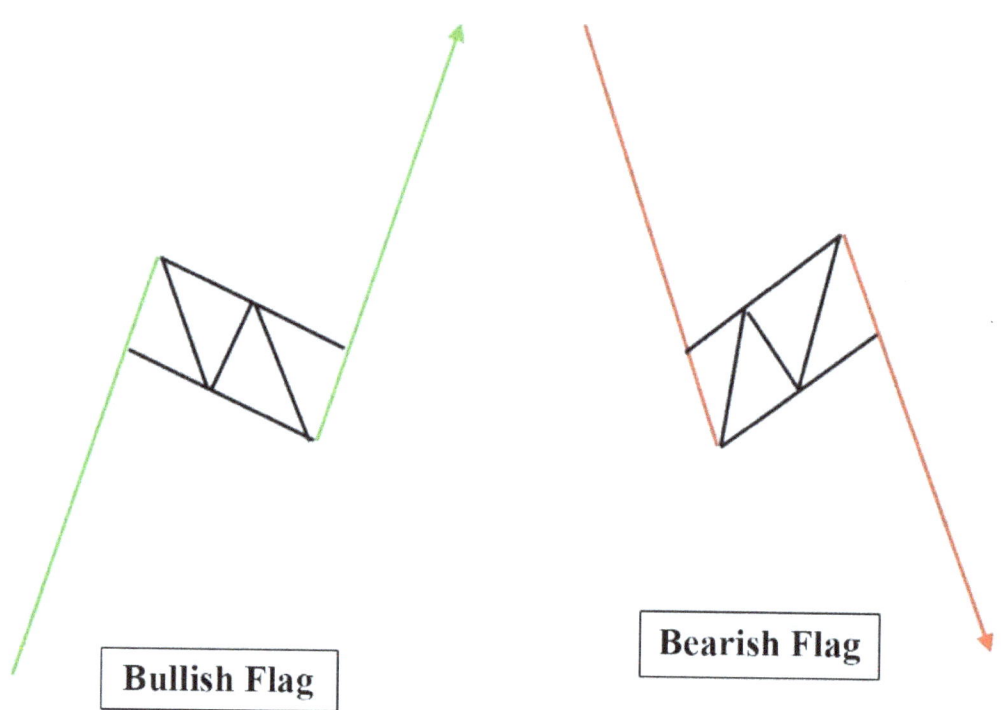

The 30-minute USDJPY chart seen below exhibits distinct formations of bullish and bearish flags. Following a period of strong upward movement in the bullish flag and a subsequent decrease in the bearish flag, the quotations get consolidated within a rectangular shape that either slopes downward or upward, creating the pattern.

Only engage in buying or selling until the price has moved outside of the pattern. To ensure optimal risk management, it is advisable to position the stop loss order slightly below or above the flag, taking into account the market's direction, whether it is bullish or bearish. The target of this pattern is to match the height of the flagpole.

V BOTTOM PATTERN

A V-shaped pattern forms when the price moves from an aggressive selling state to an aggressive buying state. This is how the pattern got its name. Because of the heavy buying that happens when a market changes direction, it can be hard to spot this trend in real time. Anyone can see this strong bullish reversal pattern on a chart, and it can happen in any market or time frame.

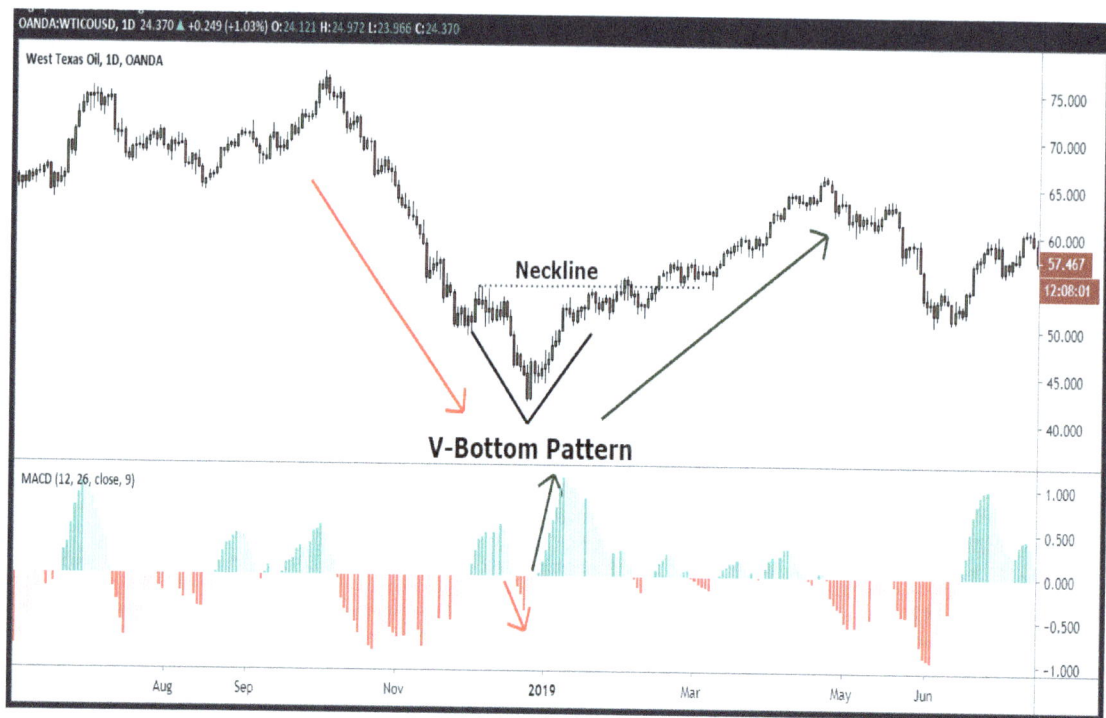

As you can see, the above figure shows a perfect V-bottom at the end of a downward trend in crude oil. Price went down until it hit a bottom, then it quickly went back up with a huge boost in energy (momentum). It is very hard to tell when a V-bottom will happen, but most traders will wait for price to break the pattern's neckline before going long when price retests the neckline.

A V-bottom is likely to happen if there is a 1-3 bar reversal and an increase in momentum and volume during the downswing that makes the low and the upswings that follows right away.

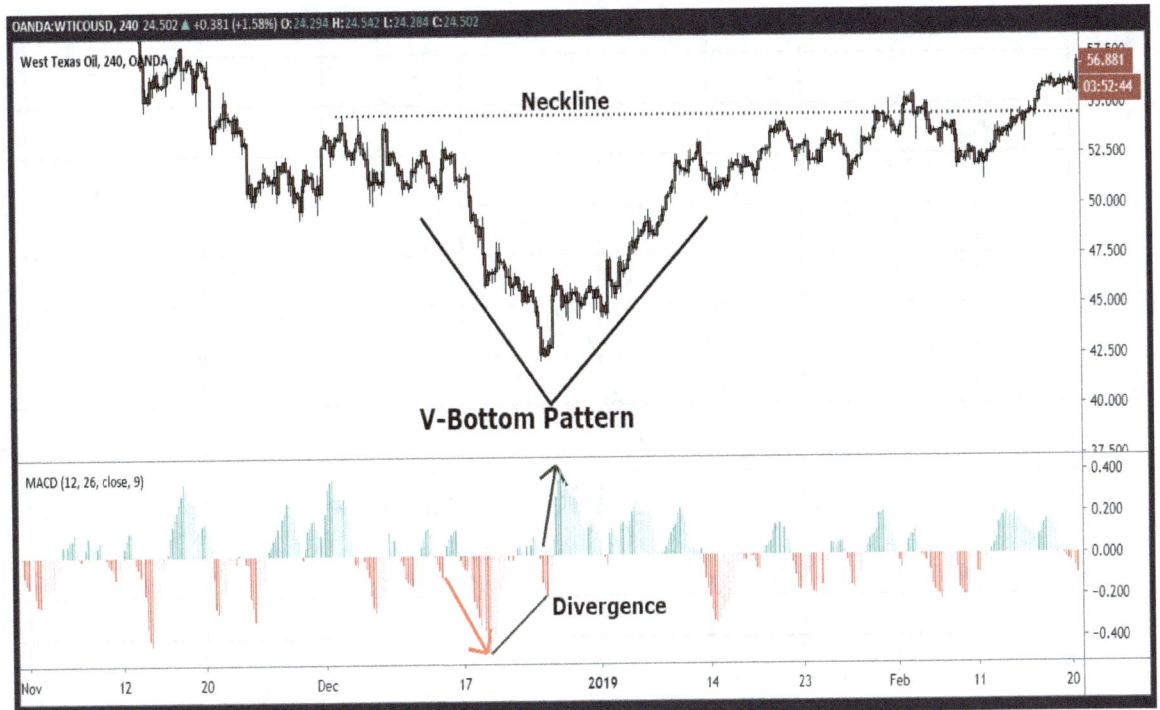

This crude oil chart for 4 hours also shows the same V-bottom shape. There was momentum difference between the MACD-Histogram's lows before the price turned up with a sharp rise in momentum, even though momentum had spiked lower at the low.

This can be another sign of a V-bottom, though it doesn't always happen. This is especially true if you start to see more buying pressure soon after. So, if you think a V-bottom is about to form, it can be very helpful to keep an eye on the price action over a number of time frames.

TRADING THE V-BOTTOM.

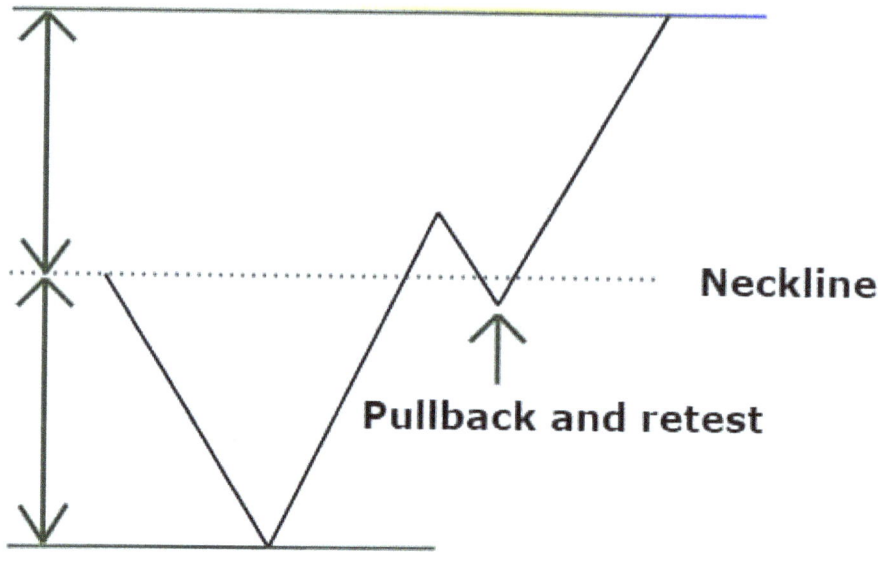

Neckline

Pullback and retest

A safe way to trade the V-bottom would be to wait for a break and close above the neckline and then try to start a long position when the price near the neckline and is turned down. Your target should be the distance between the pattern's low point and the high point of the neckline. This distance should be placed above the neckline.

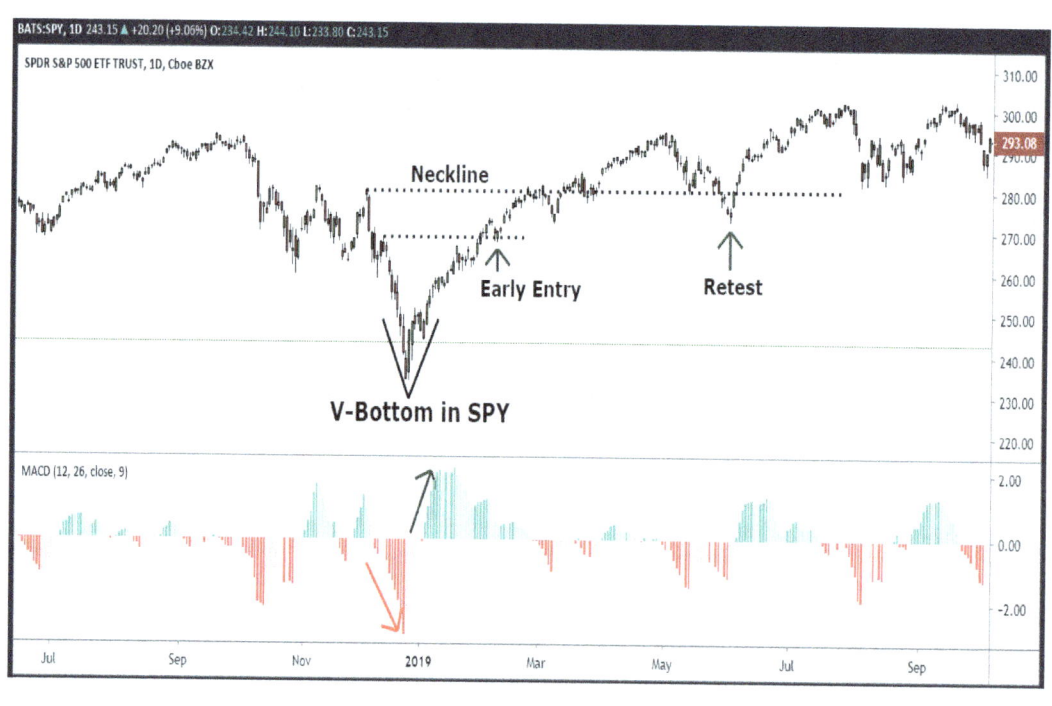

The chart above shows a V-bottom pattern that stopped SPY (S&P 500 ETF) from going down in 2018. With a lot of energy, the price fell all the way to its low point. Then it quickly turned around and started to rise again.

It may not have been clear where the neckline was, but smart traders who saw the V-bottom reversal coming early enough might have tried to open long positions using any moves that had formed during the previous selling phase.

After that V-bottom, as we all know, SPY went through another strong bullish phase and kept going up for the rest of 2019.

It can be hard to trade V-bottoms because you probably won't notice the pattern until the price goes above the neckline. However, if you pay close attention to movement and even volume, you might see it form before the neckline is broken.

The Rounding Bottom Pattern

The rounding bottom pattern has resemblance to the cup and handle pattern, the only distinction lies in the lack of a handle. This pattern emerges after a downtrend, when the selling pressure from bearish investors diminishes and the price reaches a temporary low point on the chart. At this stage, bullish investors start to exert greater influence on the market.

Following the consolidation of the asset in the side channel, the quotations breach the neckline level in an upward direction and proceed with a corrective upward movement towards the height of the pattern that has been formed.

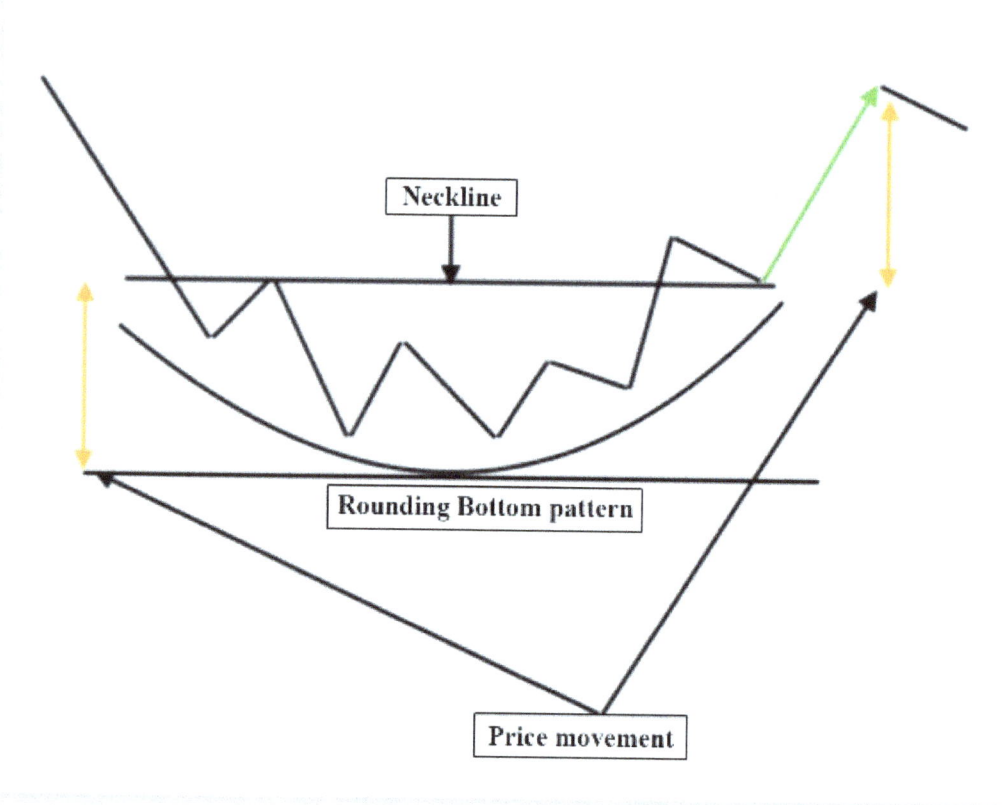

The 30-minute XAGUSD chart below illustrates the development of a rounded bottom pattern. Following the downward movement of the quotations, the asset reached a low point in the local market, which was then followed by the consolidation of the instrument. Subsequently, there is a sudden and significant increase in price, resulting in the closure of a bullish candle above the neckline level.

We might open a buy trade with the commencement of the second candle.

The objective of the movement is defined as the vertical distance between the support level and the resistance level. To mitigate potential losses, it is advisable to place the stop loss order below the level of the neckline in this particular scenario.

How to trade the rounded bottom pattern.

A target higher up that is equal to the height of the rounded bottom is frequently set by aggressive traders after a break and close above the neckline resistance level.

Most of the time, conservative traders wait to enter until the neckline has broken and closed above it, then been pulled back and tried again. Remember that the cautious entry method might not always work if the price keeps going up, and a seller might miss a good moment to buy or sell. Usually, a stop loss can be set a few pips below the swing low from before the breakout.

Watch how volume changes as this pattern forms because it often moves against the price, either going down as the pattern forms and then going up again, or going down as the price goes down.

The long-term rounded bottom pattern can be seen in both the EUR/CHF chart and the above chart. Take a look at how the EUR/CHF and NZD/CAD setups would have done with both aggressive and cautious entry strategies. In this case, the volume also dropped sharply as the chart pattern formed. Even after the price hit the bottom, the volume stayed low, which was a sign that selling pressure would ease and the price would likely go up.

When volume acts like it did in the cases above, rounding bottom patterns indicate that an upward trend is likely to change direction. If you are short on the market and see this trend again, be careful or get ready to go long when it stops.

The Double Top Pattern

The double top pattern frequently appears in candlestick charts of both higher and lower time frames. The asset is exhibiting a double top pattern as it trades within a channel bounded by the resistance and support levels.

Following a failed second effort to breach the resistance line, the quotations reverse direction and successfully surpass the neckline, which represents the upper support level.

Following a successful breach and subsequent retesting of the recently established resistance level, the price continues to advance, so fully completing the creation of the pattern.

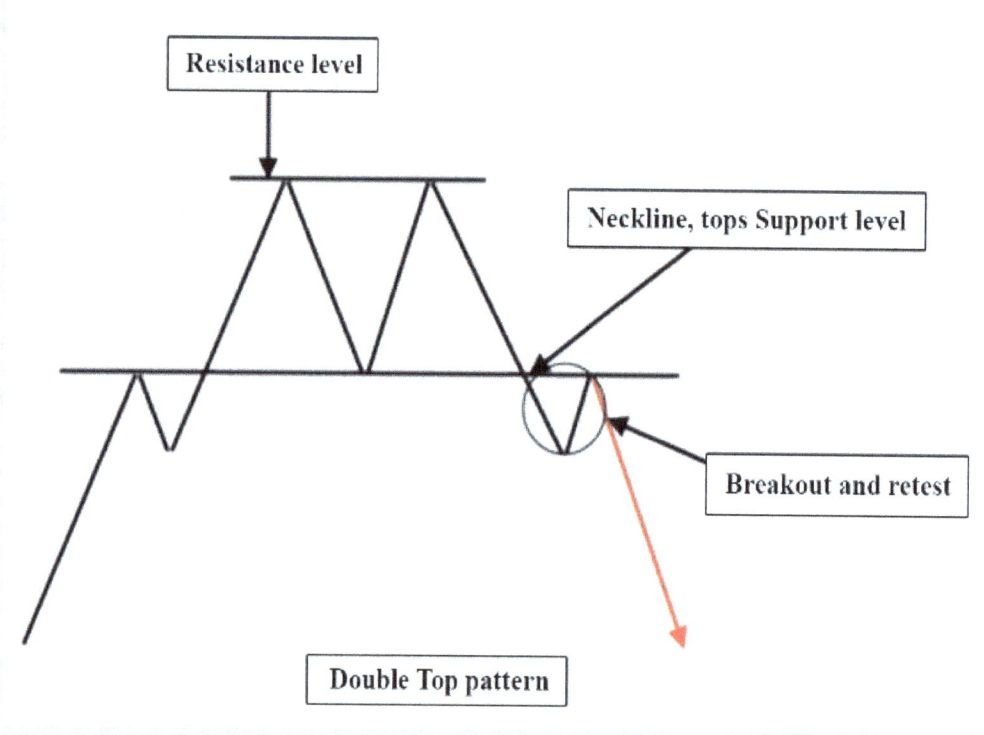

An excellent illustration of this pattern may be observed in the 30-minute USCRUDE chart provided below. The chart depicts the emergence of two peaks and a sudden breakout of their support level. Additionally, there is a consolidation of the tool mentioned before and a subsequent re-evaluation of the newly established resistance. The entry point is situated under the level of support. Subsequently, a prudent objective is computed based on principles of financial management.

The target size is equivalent to the vertical distance between the highest support level and the resistance level. To mitigate potential losses, traders should place a stop loss order above the support level.

The double top pattern is observable across many time frames and serves as a key instrument in a trader's arsenal for detecting possible market reversals.

The Double Bottom Pattern

The double bottom pattern is a reversal pattern that indicates the start of a new trend, contrasting with the double top pattern. Typically, it happens inside the local asset base and tests the support level on two occasions.

The formation of this pattern entails a breach of the resistance level, followed by a further retest of the breached resistance by the quotations. Subsequently, the price ascends to the level of the height of the side channel, which was created by the support and resistance lines.

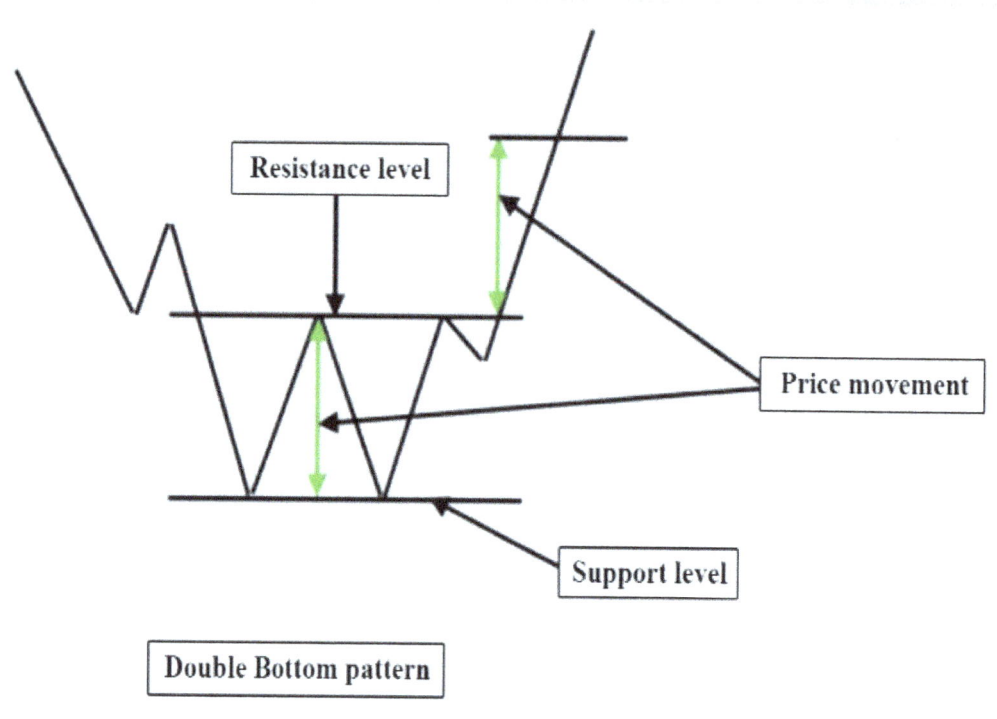

An illustration of this recurring sequence may be observed in the 30-minute ETHUSD chart. The chart depicted below illustrates the process of pattern formation. Following the establishment of the second bottom, the asset swiftly moved towards the resistance level, successfully surpassing it and subsequently retesting it, therefore consolidating at a higher level.

Following the consolidation of the instrument above the resistance, we may initiate a buy trade. The price fluctuations correspond to the magnitude of the lateral range formed by the support and resistance lines.

The trade has the potential to be terminated at two specific moments. To adhere to risk management principles, it is advisable to position the stop loss at a lower level in this particular scenario.

THE THREE-BOTTOM PATTERNS

The Triple Bottom pattern builds on the Double Bottom design. Before the final break, price patterns on a triple bottom show that there were several failed attempts to break through areas of support and resistance. A triple bottom has been made when the price breaks above the last move high. This is something that traders often look for.

The triple bottom is a symbol of a bullish reversal in the price chart. It could mean that buyers (bulls) are taking over and sellers (bears) are losing control of a decline.

The above chart shows a triple bottom pattern, it means that the EUR/GBP pair has turned upward after going down. After the initial low, the price went back down and made a swing high. This was followed by another drop that ended near the initial low.

After that, price made a second swing low that was almost as high as the first swing high. It then went back down again, but it couldn't break below the two previous bottoms.

Traders often wait for price to break above the last swing high before they are sure that a triple bottom has formed. Most of the time, the next move up will be the start of a new upswing (swing high).

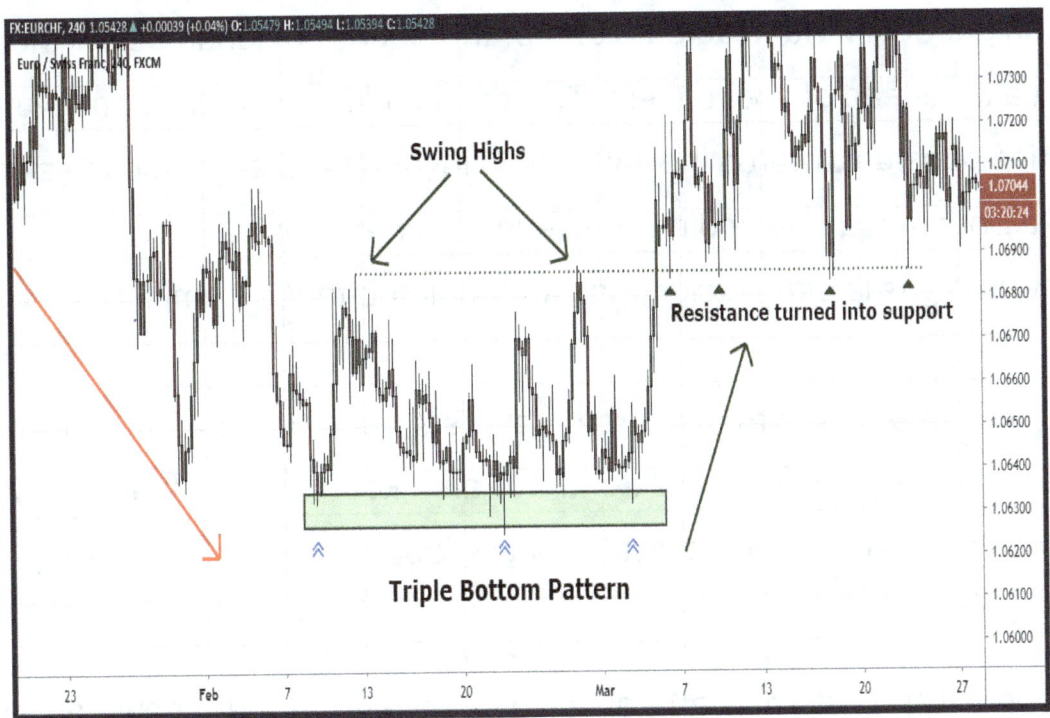

This second chart shows a triple bottom that is a little more complicated than the first one. The EUR/CHF 4-hour period. Pay attention to how many times the price tried to close below the first bottom while it was trying that price range. The wicks that were left behind show that the sellers lost control of the market. The more they tried to sell, the more the bulls fought back. Eventually, the sellers gave up, and the price started to go up.

Also, keep in mind that the two swing highs were about the same height. Even though it's not always necessary, this is a strong sign that a triple bottom may be about to complete because price fell a third time but couldn't break through that level.

The inverted head and shoulders pattern are not the same as triple tops, even though it may look like them superficially. Inverse head and shoulders patterns are traded like triple bottoms when price breaks above the previous swing highs while the middle bottom of the pattern extends below the other two peaks instead of above them. Traders should keep an eye on volume as the price goes up towards the swing high level. This is a good early sign that a triple bottom may be ending. A rise in volume before a price break above the swing highs is often a sign that your triple bottom is complete.

The triple bottom pattern is a strong reversal pattern that will not only show you a possible change in the trend but also keep you on the right side of price action if your volume indicator backs it up.

TRIPPLE TOP PATTERN

The Triple Top Pattern is a bearish reversal pattern that shows up after a long period of uptrend. It means that the market's mood might change from Bullish to bearish.

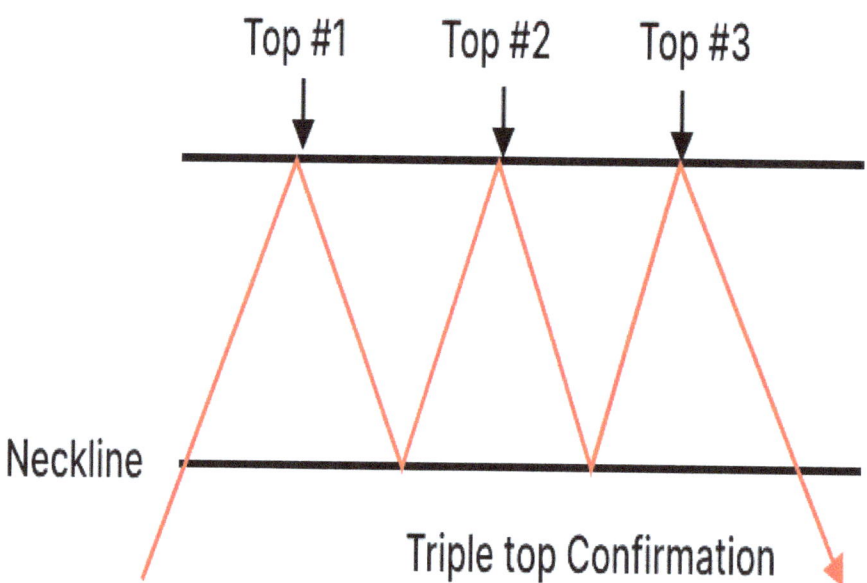

If you see a Triple Top Pattern, it means that buyers are losing strength and sellers are gaining strength. The first peak shows that bullish buyers have run out of money, which causes a small drop. The next rise, on the other hand, fails to break the previous high, creating the second peak. This failure makes the support level stronger and brings in buyers who are willing to sell. The price goes back down, but the next rise fails to break through the resistance level a third time, creating the third peak. At this point, sellers have more power than buyers, which causes a big drop and often a change in the direction.

Why The Triple Top Is Important?

Traders and buyers are interested in the Triple Top Pattern because it gives them useful information about how markets work. Traders can predict when a trend might change by noticing this pattern and making changes to their trading methods as needed. It lets traders get out of long positions or even open short positions to profit from the next move down. When used with other technical patterns, the Triple Top Pattern can also be used to confirm a trend change, making it more likely to happen.

How to Find the Triple Top Pattern.

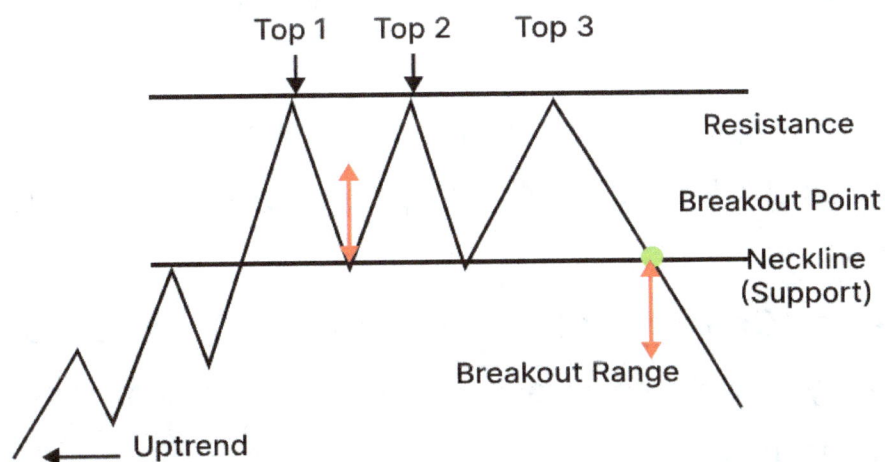

To see the Triple Top Pattern, you need to pay close attention to price movement and chart patterns. To find this pattern, traders often use basic tools such as trendlines, support and resistance levels, and oscillators. Some basic steps you can take to find the Triple Top Pattern are outlined below:

- Find a price trend that has been going up for a long time.
- Look for three peaks that are close to the same height and make a resistance level that is either flat or slightly sloped downwards.
- Two small pullbacks between the peaks will help you confirm the pattern.
- Look at the amount of trading that happened when the pattern was forming. Less activity can mean that people are no longer interested in buying.

Using Triple Top Patterns to Trade

To make the most money when trading the Triple Top Pattern, you need to carefully consider when to enter and leave the trade. When you trade this pattern, here are some important things to remember:

- **Entry Strategy:** Traders usually wait for the price to drop below the support level, which shows that the pattern is over. When this happens, it's time to get short options.
- **Stop-Loss Orders:** Putting a stop-loss order above the barrier level can help you avoid losing too much if the pattern doesn't work and the price goes up.

- **Take-Profit Levels:** Traders can set take-profit levels by figuring out how high the pattern is and placing it below the point where it broke out. Support levels or swing lows from the past can also be used as possible goals.

The Bullish Hammer Pattern

A bullish hammer is a technical analysis pattern that indicates a potential reversal in a downtrend. The hammer pattern is a bullish reversal indicator in Japanese candlestick analysis. The hammer candlestick is considered one of the most effective patterns for intraday trading.

This hammer pattern emerges at a specific low point and indicates the prevailing influence of buyers in the market. When engaging in trading using this particular pattern, it is crucial for a trader to concentrate on the overall market conditions.

If the downward movement was strong before the emergence of the hammer, there is a significant likelihood that the subsequent pattern will result in a bullish reversal and a similarly forceful movement. Furthermore, while engaging in trading using this particular pattern, it is imperative to start the process from established support and resistance levels in order to ascertain the price dynamics with greater precision.

The color of the hammer is inconsequential, but, the fundamental composition of the bar is crucial. Conversely, a green candle, often known as a bullish candle, signifies a greater level of purchasing strength. This pattern derives its name from its distinctive form, resembling that of a hammer, characterized by a tiny body and a long downward wick.

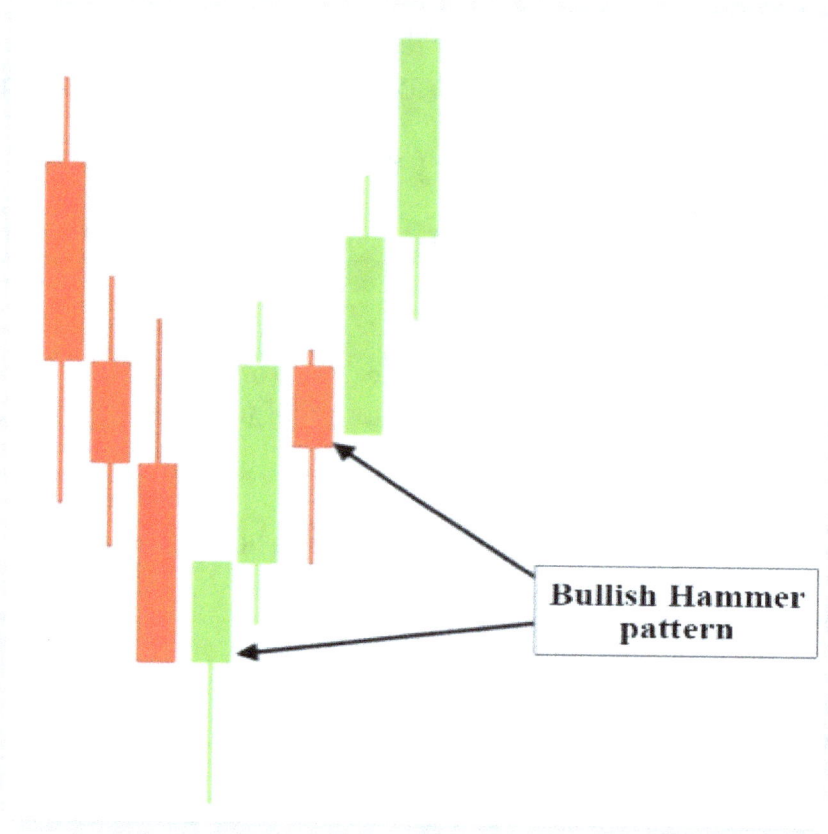

Bullish Hammer pattern

On the 15-minute chart for the CADJPY currency pair, there is a signal that occurred during the day. The presence of a hammer reversal pattern indicates the existence of a support level for the asset, which acts as a barrier preventing bears from pushing the price below it.

The resistance marks the start of the fall. The significant negative trend necessitated a correspondingly robust rebound in the form of a strong rising movement. In the chart provided below, a sequence of bullish hammer formations emerged, resulting in a subsequent reversal of the quotations.

A buy trade may have been executed following the emergence of the second hammer pattern. Position the stop loss order just below the lowest point of pattern.

THE HEAD AND SHOULDER PATTERN

The occurrence of the head and shoulders reversal pattern on charts is less common compared to other chart patterns. It creates three vertices, with one positioned centrally above the other two. The neckline, which serves as the support level, is located at the foot of these peaks.

Initiate sell trades once the right shoulder has formed, the neckline level has been breached by quotations descending from the top, and the price has consolidated at a lower level. Furthermore, it is recommended that the right shoulder be positioned somewhat higher than the left shoulder, but this may not always be the case.

If a breakout occurs, there is a possibility of a temporary upward reversal to assess the recently formed resistance. The price movement are determined by measuring the distance between the neckline level and the head.

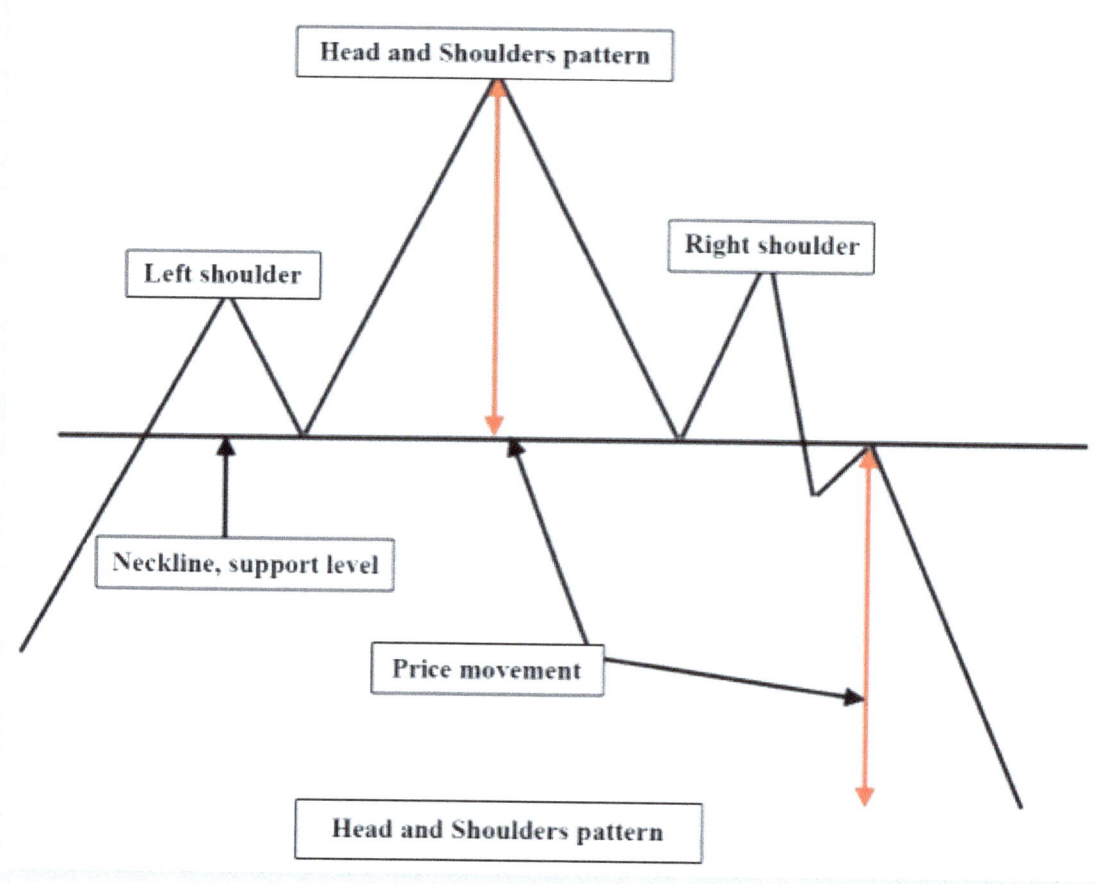

The provided BTCUSD chart displays a complete and traditional head and shoulders pattern within a 15-minute timeframe. Once the price dropped below the neckline and the quotes consolidated below this level, we may consider selling the instrument.

To determine the take-profit level, one can calculate the distance between the neck level and the head level. To mitigate potential losses, it is advisable to position the stop loss only slightly above the breached support level in this particular scenario.

THE WEDGE PATTERN

There are several variations of the wedge. This pattern can occur in both bullish and bearish movements.

A rising wedge pattern observed in both uptrends and downtrends indicates an impending reversal of the quotations towards a downward trend. In both instances, the descending wedge pattern suggests an impending breach of the upper trendline. When initiating trades using this pattern, it is crucial to pay attention to the height of the formation.

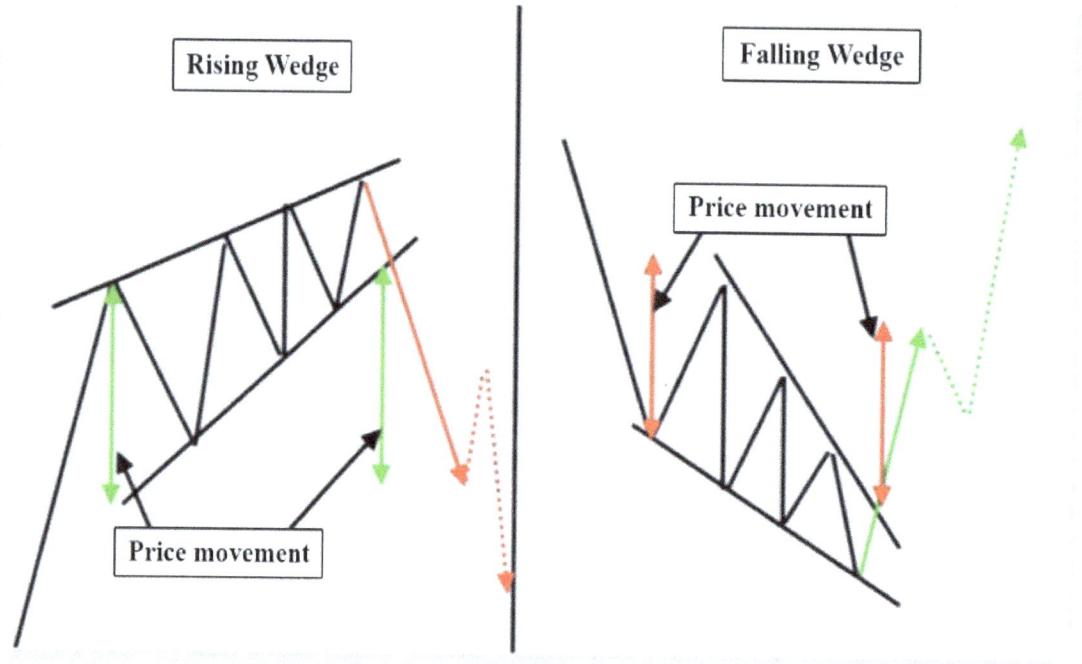

An illustration of the development of this pattern may be observed in the 30-minute GBPAUD chart. The chart below illustrates that as the trade channel contracted and the wedge pattern emerged, there was a significant downward movement in the price, reaching the same distance as the height of the pattern.

Enter the market only after a firm consolidation of the price and a significant increase in trading volumes. To effectively manage risk, it is advisable to place the stop loss order either above or below the breached level, taking into account the specific characteristics of the pattern.

The Falling Wedge Pattern

A falling wedge is a technical chart pattern that occurs when the price of an asset is gradually decreasing inside a narrowing range. The falling wedge is a type of continuation pattern that has resemblance to the triangle chart pattern.

Consequently, inexperienced day traders frequently commit errors while initiating trades. The primary distinction between a falling wedge and ascending or descending triangles is in the downward trajectory of the support and resistance lines, as opposed to the clearly horizontal support or resistance line found in a triangle.

As a component of risk management, price movement should be precisely specified as the vertical extent of the wedge formation. Nevertheless, in the event of a substantial surge in trading volumes, quotations may ascend much more.

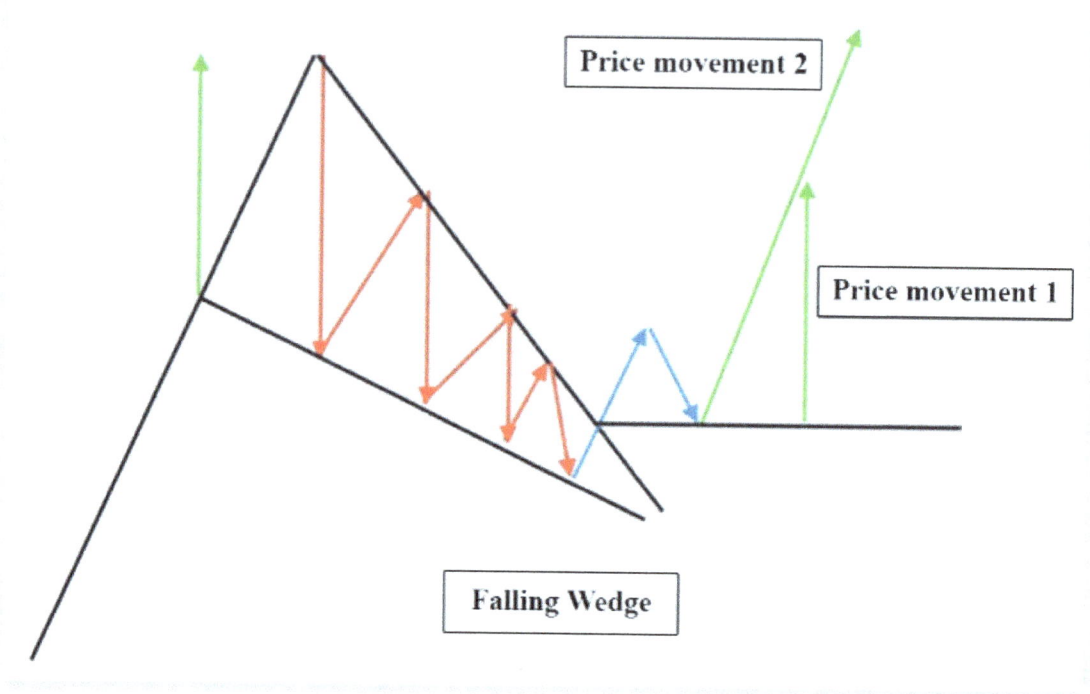

An illustration of the descending wedge chart patterns may be observed in the 15-minute chart of Apple Inc. The chart illustrates a slow decrease in price following a previous bullish trend, with both the lows and highs of the price declining.

Following the contraction of the trading channel, there was a sudden upward movement in the breakdown of quotes. Once the broken resistance line has been re-tested, we may initiate a buy trade with a target set at the height of the falling wedge.

To mitigate potential losses, it is advisable to establish a stop loss at the bottom boundary of the trading channel.

How to Trade the Falling Wedge Pattern

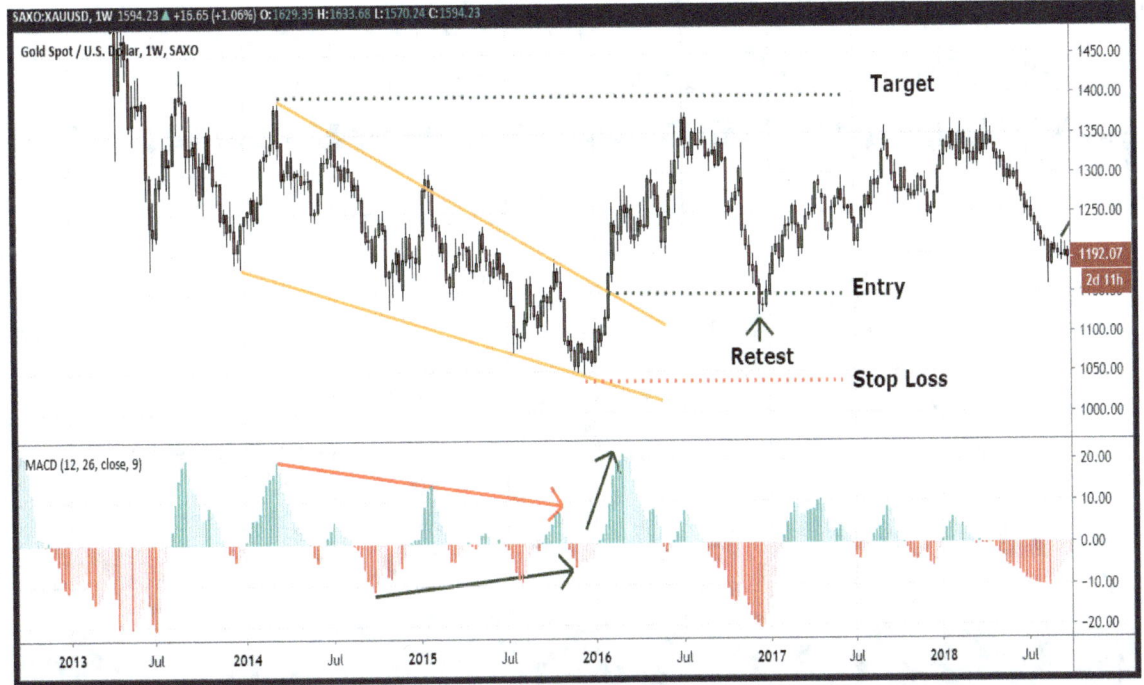

It is common for aggressive traders to wait for price to cross above the upper support line before opening a long position. This is because the falling wedge is a bullish chart pattern. On the other hand, buyers who are careful will often wait before going long until the price has had a chance to test the upper support line again. You should remember that a retest of the breakout level might not always happen, which means a trader might miss an entry.

Having a stop loss a few pips below the previous low point before the breakout. The top level where the falling wedge began is the best spot to set a profit target.

If you are watching a falling wedge in real time, you might want to look for momentum divergence on a MACD-Histogram between the lower lows. This can be used as an extra sign that the falling wedge may be ending soon. This pattern will usually end once price breaks above the support line, and momentum will usually pick up. Don't forget that the above case shows a drop in the MACD-Histogram's peaks before the pattern stops. This doesn't always happen, but if it does, it's another sign to look out for because the MACD-Histogram also showed a wedge-shaped pattern.

The falling wedge in gold can be seen in the chart above, which ends with a trend continuation. This is a great example of how careful traders would not have been able to join until the breakout level was tested again.

On the other hand, the MACD-Histogram began to show momentum difference between the lower lows at the support line. This was more proof that the falling wedge was about to end.

Also, look at how the pattern finished when the price went above the resistance line. This made the movement go up very quickly. A stop loss could have been put below the lowest lower low, and the target could have been set at the first point where the rising wedge showed up.

You should always make sure that the possible reward is greater than the risk you are willing to take. If your stop loss is too far away, you might want to move it below a swing long that formed on the way up before the resistance line was broken.

A falling wedge is a bullish pattern that can show up during a trend either going up or down (uptrend or downtrend). If you are on short position on your chosen market and see this pattern again, be careful. If you are long, get ready for a chance to go long.

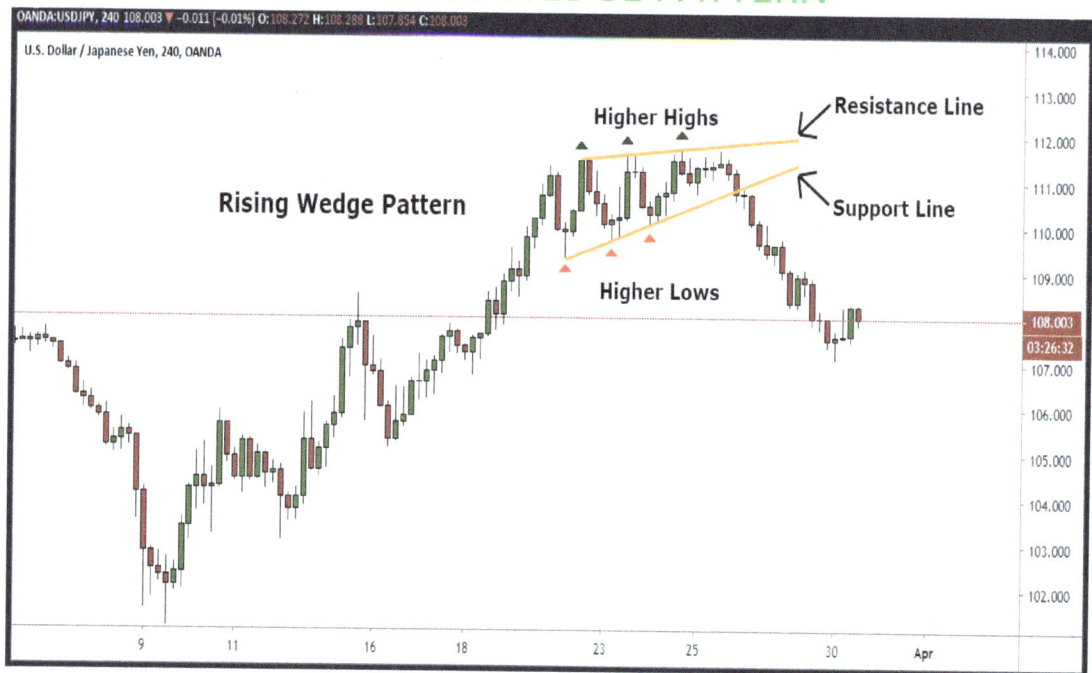

You can see the rising wedge pattern a lot of the time in all markets and time frames. In a downtrend, this chart pattern can be seen as a trend continuation pattern. In an uptrend, it can be seen as a bearish reversal pattern.

There are a series of higher lows (support) and higher highs (resistance) in a rising wedge. These ranges get smaller and smaller until the price breaks below support and the trend changes. The lower support line has a higher ascending slope than the upper resistance line. This is another thing that makes a rising wedge stand out.

As you can see in the above chart, the AUD/USD pair formed a rising wedge pattern while it was going down. It was more than two years before this pattern was broken, and the old decline started up again.

Trading with the Rising Wedge Pattern.

The rising wedge is a bearish pattern, so traders who want to make money usually wait for price to cross below the lower support line before they go short. On the other hand, traders who want to be safe will usually wait to open a short position until price has had a chance to test the lower support line from below again. Remember that this might not always happen, which could cause a seller to miss an entry.

A stop loss a few pips above the last high before the breakout will work well. The best place to set a target is at the lower level where the rising wedge started.

If you are watching a rising wedge in real time, it might be helpful to look for momentum divergence on a MACD-Histogram between the higher highs. This can be used as an extra sign that a rising wedge may be ending soon.

The AUD/USD chart above formed the same multi-year rising wedge that I showed in my last chart. Keep in mind, though, that even though the price hit higher highs, the pace started to slow down between each peak. This is a common occurrence for these trends.

This is yet another great example of price going back to the support line, trying it again from below, and then going down. There was another chance to set a target with a stop loss above the previous higher high at the start of the rising wedge.

Always make sure that the possible reward is greater than the risk you are taking. If your stop loss is too far away, you might want to move it above a swing high that was made on the way down, before the support line was broken.

If you see this pattern on your chosen market, be careful if you are long or get ready for a shorting chance. This pattern is bearish and can show up during either an uptrend or a downturn.

THE DIAMOND BOTTOM PATTERN

Technical experts see the diamond bottom pattern as a strong sign of a bullish reversal, even though it doesn't happen very often. Before narrowing into a smaller range, this bullish reversal pattern gets wider from the left. It stays that way until price breaks out above the resistance line, which completes the pattern.

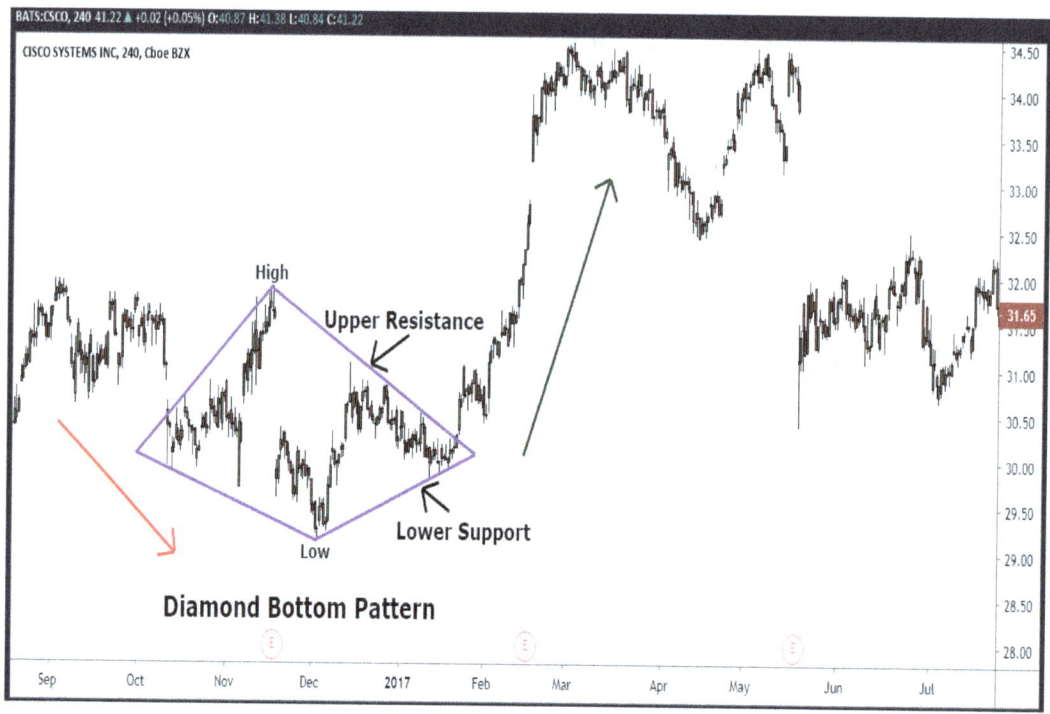

The word "diamond bottom" refers to a pattern in which prices rise first and then fall. Trendlines are used to describe this pattern.

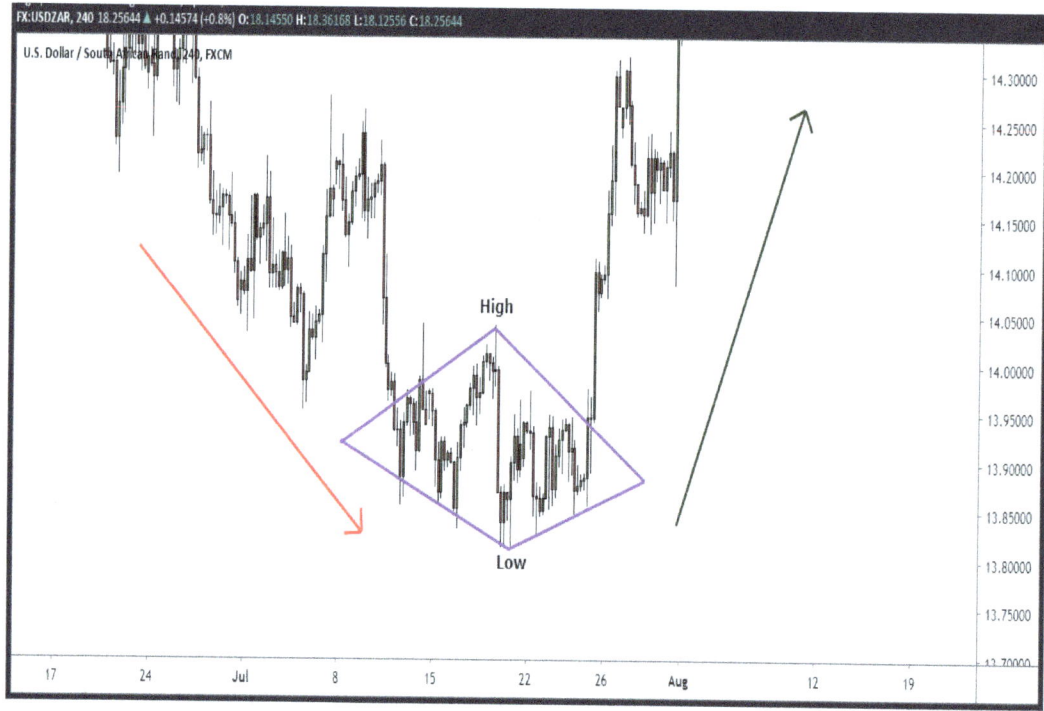

Here is another example of a diamond bottom that showed up at the bottom of a downtrend and was followed by a strong change in the trend to the upside when the pattern was finished. One reason technical traders like the diamond pattern is that it shows how quickly prices can move after the pattern ends.

How to Trade with a Diamond Bottom.

The USD/ZAR pair and the stochastic indicator can be seen on this 4-hour chart.

Traders will often go long using our previous diamond top pattern and set a target level equal to the height of the diamond shape when price breaks above the upper trendline resistance.

Most of the time, you can place a stop loss a few pips below the last move low that happened before the breakout.

Before you take a trade, it's always a good idea to wait for a second confirmation cue. This is true for most chart patterns. This will make it more likely that the pattern will end in a straight line and that the price will reach your profit target.

One of these tools is the stochastic oscillator, which can show a change in price movement before a rise. Pay attention to how the stochastic oscillator crossed up before the price broke through the resistance line. This caused the price to go through the roof and quickly hit the first target.

This chart goes all the way back to the first diamond bottom formation in Cisco stock. Before the price went up, the stochastic oscillator showed more proof of the diamond bottom pattern that had formed at the end of the decline. Your stop loss would have been very tight if you had traded this setup. This would have given you a great risk-to-reward ratio. Pay attention to how fast the price went up.

As a trader, one of the most important things to think about is your risk versus your possible gain (risk to reward ratio). As you can see from the chart above, you could also set an initial target at the high of the diamond pattern after the breakout and a stop loss below the better low from earlier. This is a different way to find a starting place, but it needs to make sense in terms of the risks and reward.

Even though it doesn't happen very often, the diamond bottom pattern can lead to a bullish reversal with a clear target and stop loss level. If you see this trend again, you should think about trading it because it can help you make a lot of money.

The Pennant Pattern

The pennant Pattern has resemblance to the flag pattern. The distinction between the pennant and the flag lies in the fact that the former assumes the shape of a symmetrical triangle. Regarding the flag, the price range of movement is determined by the whole length of the flagpole. While, the pennant, the price movement corresponds to the distance measured from the lowest point to the beginning of the symmetrical triangular formation.

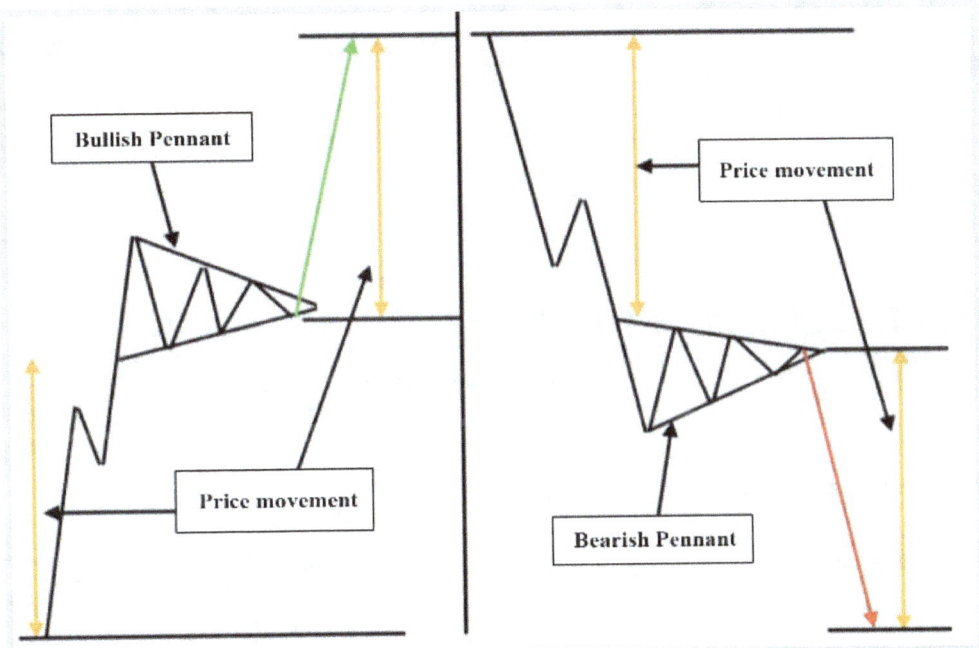

The provided chart below displays a 15-minute timeframe for the XRPUSD pair, showcasing a visual representation of both a bullish and bearish pennant. For both scenarios, the price range of the movement is equivalent to the vertical distance between the support or resistance level and the initial formation of a triangle pattern. In both scenarios, the entry points occur when the price exits the triangular formation.

Position the stop loss either above or below the established pattern, according on the direction of movement.

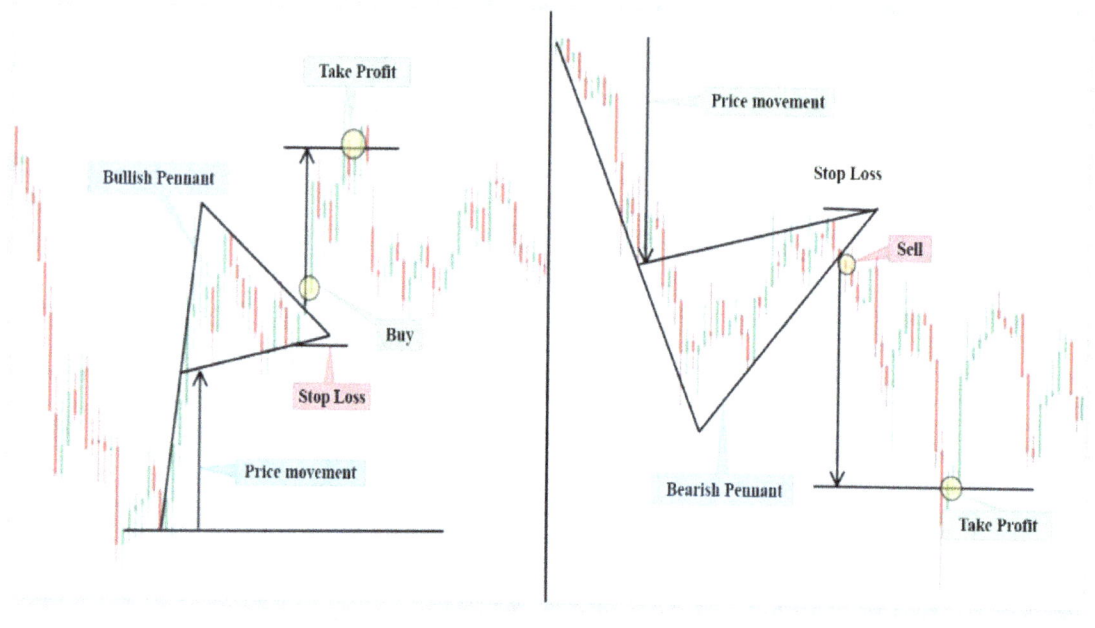

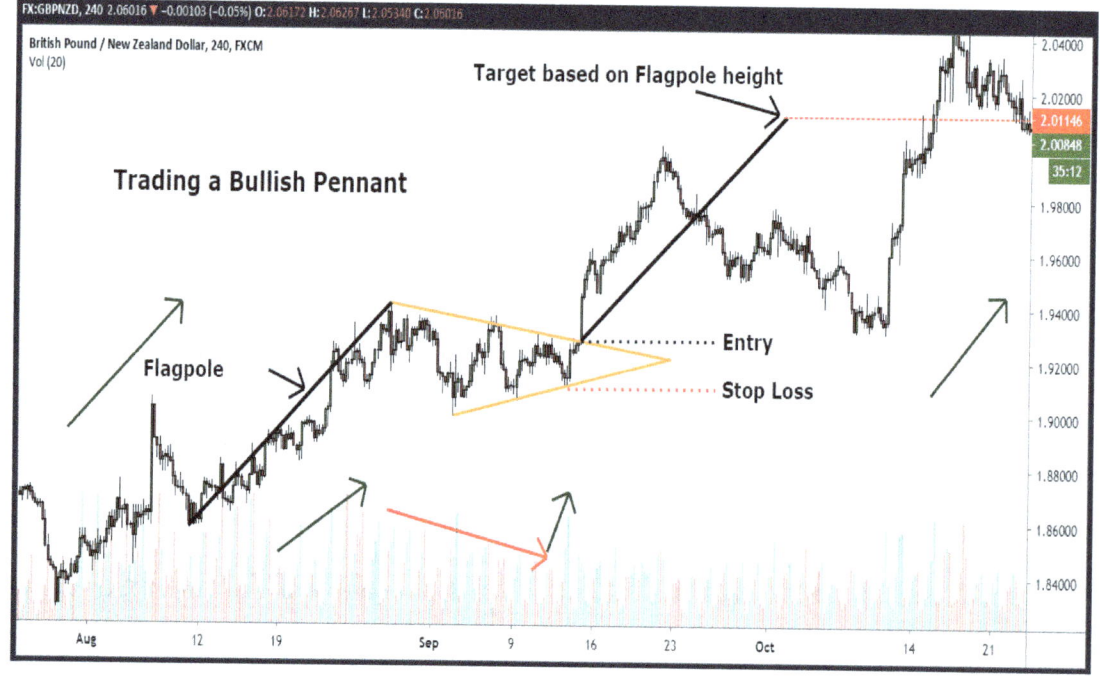

TRADING WITH THE PENNANT PATTERN

As we saw with the previous bearish pennant pattern, traders often open a long position once price breaks above the upper trendline support and sets a profit target level equal to the height of the flagpole. A few pip(s) below the last move low before the breakout is a good place to put a stop loss.

Both bullish and bearish pennant patterns will usually show certain traits as they form. These traits can help a trader figure out if this pattern will be a good opportunity to make enough profit.

The first thing that should be done is to watch how volume changes before and after the flag forms. When the volume goes up during the flagpole phase and down during the pennant phase, that's a good sign.

Second, the pennant shape shouldn't go back and forth over more than half of the flagpole. If it does, you might be looking at a triangle instead of a pennant. Last but not least, a rise in volume before the breakout is often a good sign that the pattern has finished.

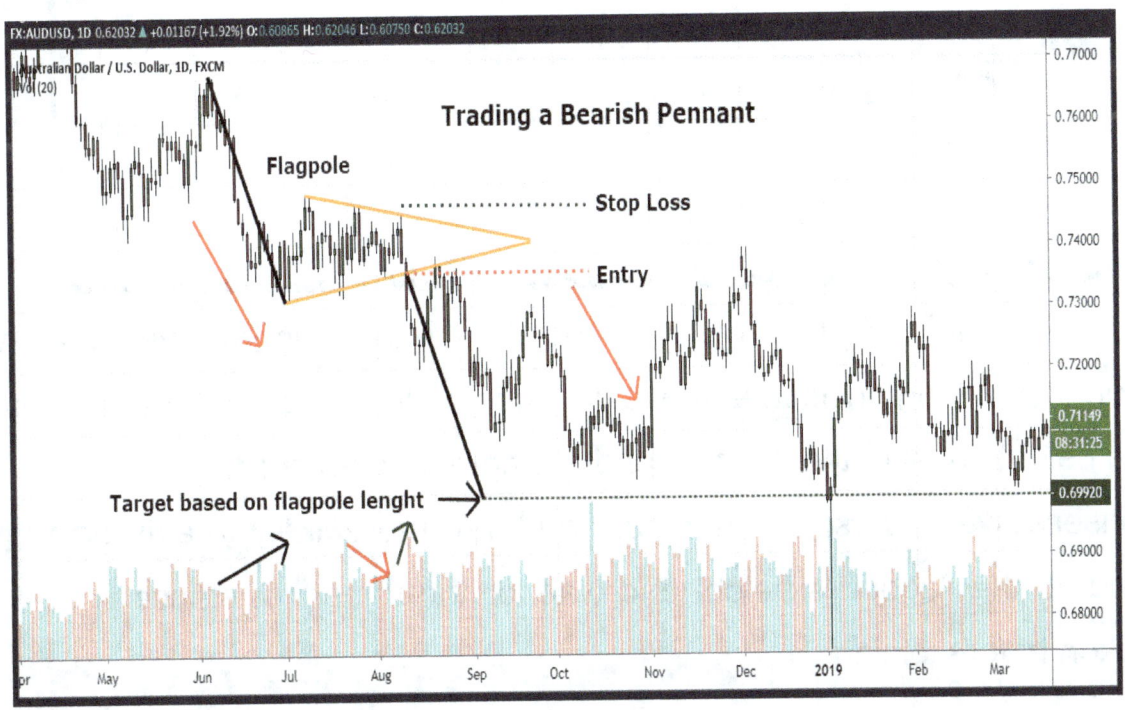

Looking at this chart above the same bearish AUD/USD pennant pattern that I showed before has the same volume and retracement features.

Keep in mind that bearish pennant patterns don't always show a clear drop in volume during the pennant formation. This is because bearish markets tend to move faster because of the fear and worry that fuel a sell-off. In the above case, the volume didn't start to go down until the very end of the pattern's formation.

TRADING WITH THE FLAG PATTERN.

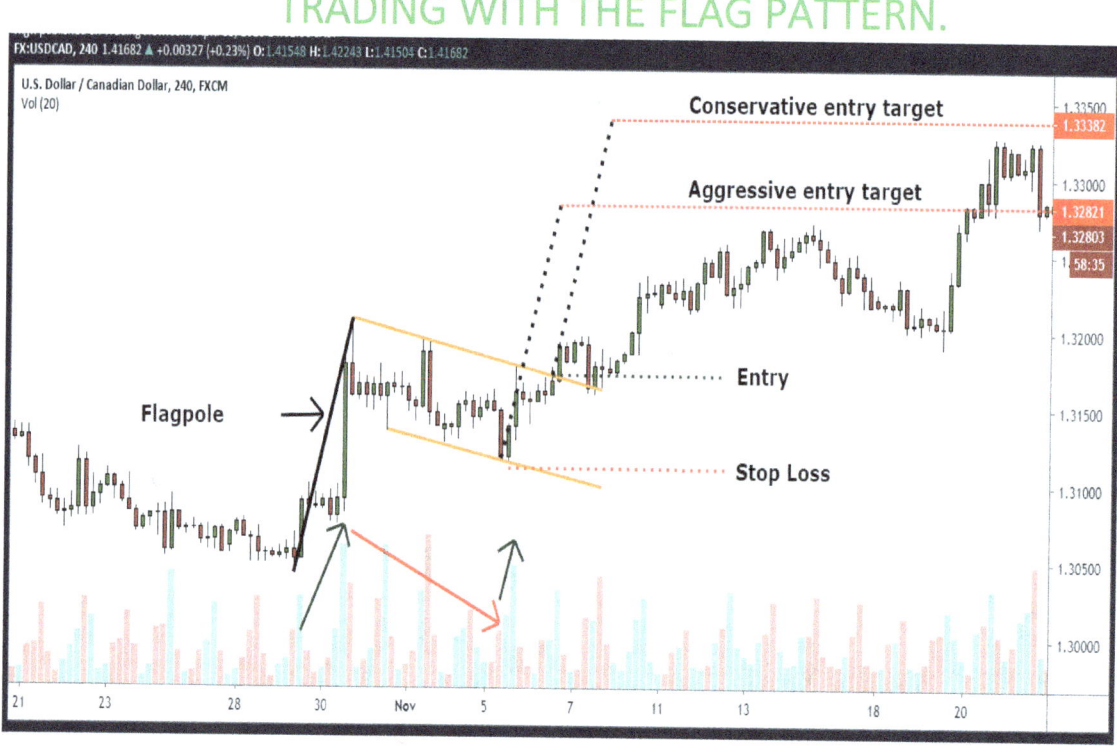

Using the bullish flag pattern, we talked about earlier, aggressive traders will often start a long position at the lower support line. They will set their target at a height equal to the flagpole above where they entered.

Conservative traders, on the other hand, are more likely to aim for a level equal to the flagpole's height and wait for the upper resistance line to be broken before joining.

What a trader should know is that as the pattern forms, it will usually show a few traits that can help them figure out if it will be a good time to trade.

First, pay attention to how the volumes changes before and during the flag creation. When the volume goes up during the pennant phase and down during the flag phase, that's a good sign.

Additionally, the flag pattern shouldn't go back and forth more than half of the shaft. If it does, you may not even be working with a pattern.

Finally, a rise in volume before the breakout is often a good sign that the pattern was finished.

This last chart shows the same bearish AUD/NZD flag pattern that we talked about before. It has the same volume and retracing features. The target would have been reached with either the aggressive or the conservative entry strategy.

Because fear and worry drive sell-offs, bearish markets tend to move faster. This means that bearish flag patterns won't always show a drop-in volume during the formation of the flag. This behavior can sometimes make the breakout phase noise go up less obviously.

The flag pattern is a strong trend continuation pattern that can be seen in all markets and timeframes. This is why technical traders like it so much: the end of these trends often leads to a strong move that gets you to your profit target quickly.

Trading Strategies Based on Patterns for Short-Term and Intraday Trading.

All of the aforementioned chart patterns may be utilized for day trading methods. Optimal time intervals for doing market analysis are 5 mins timeframe, 15 mins timeframe and 30-minute timeframe respectively. For a brief investing strategy lasting 1-2 days, the hourly chart might be utilized.

Displayed below is a 5-minute chart of the EURUSD currency pair, illustrating the creation of a bullish flag pattern. Upon analyzing the price movement using the flagpole pattern and observing the price's exit from the pattern, I initiated a trade to purchase a minimum of 0.01 lots, with a predetermined target for the instrument.

I placed a stop loss order within the flag pattern at the exact point that the upward movement started. After thirty minutes, the trade concluded with a $1.62. profit.

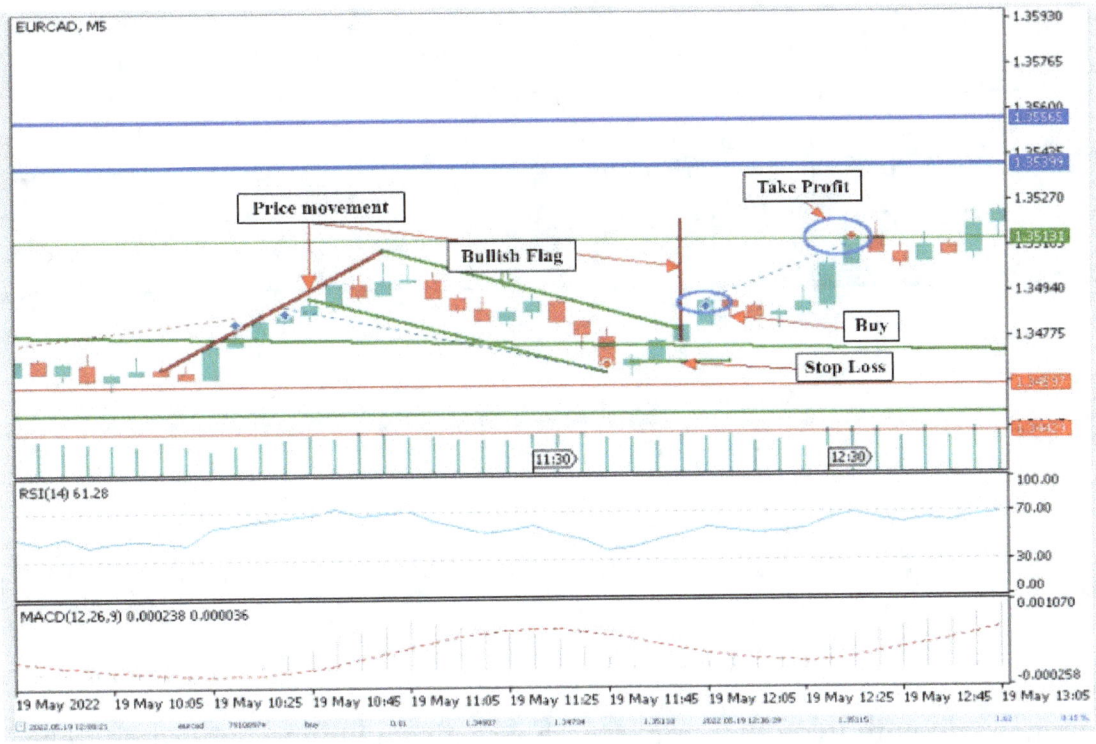

Upon doing an analysis of the 15-minute GBPUSD chart, I observed the formation of a descending wedge pattern, indicating an anticipated breakout in quotations.

Upon the price breaking through and then testing the level, I initiated a buy trade with a volume of 0.01 lots.

As part of the trading strategy, the objective for the instrument was set at the distance between the start of the downtrend and the start of the first upward correction. Then the stop loss was strategically placed below the breached level as a component of the risk management strategy. After a period of time, the trade concluded during the same day, resulting in 6.52 dollars profit of.

Simultaneously with two other trade, there was also a buying opportunity observed in the 30-minute EURUSD chart. An instrument has generated a symmetrical triangular pattern. Allow me to reiterate that in the context of the trading method using a symmetrical triangle pattern, the price has the potential to move in either an upward or downward direction. Hence, it is necessary to await a confirmation of the breakdown.

Furthermore, a bullish hammer materialized at the foundation of the triangle prior to the commencement of upward movement, serving as supplementary validation of the buyers' strength. The impulsive breakthrough of the triangle resulted in the formation of another confirming pattern known as the bullish flag.

Upon the completion of the flag pattern, I initiated a buy trade with a volume of 0.01 lots, while setting a target equal to the vertical distance of the flagpole. A stop loss order was positioned below the flag pattern that was created. The objective was achieved 1hour 30 minutes later after initiating the trade, resulting in a profit of 3.14 dollars.

Day Trading Charts Patterns.

I can only speak from my own trading experience the best patterns for day trading are: The Bullish and Bearish Flag Pattern, Rectangle Pattern, Pennant and Wedges Patterns.

Follow these five step-by-step directions when trading any of the chart patterns:

1. **Always check to see if the market is moving in a direction (Trending) or staying the same (consolidating).**

In spite of the fact that some of these simple chart patterns look like consolidation, this step is very important because they actually show the continuation of an underlying trend.

The bullish flag pattern forms after a stock price has gone up significantly. In the pattern itself, there is only a short break from the main trend, or consolidation, before it breaks to new highs.

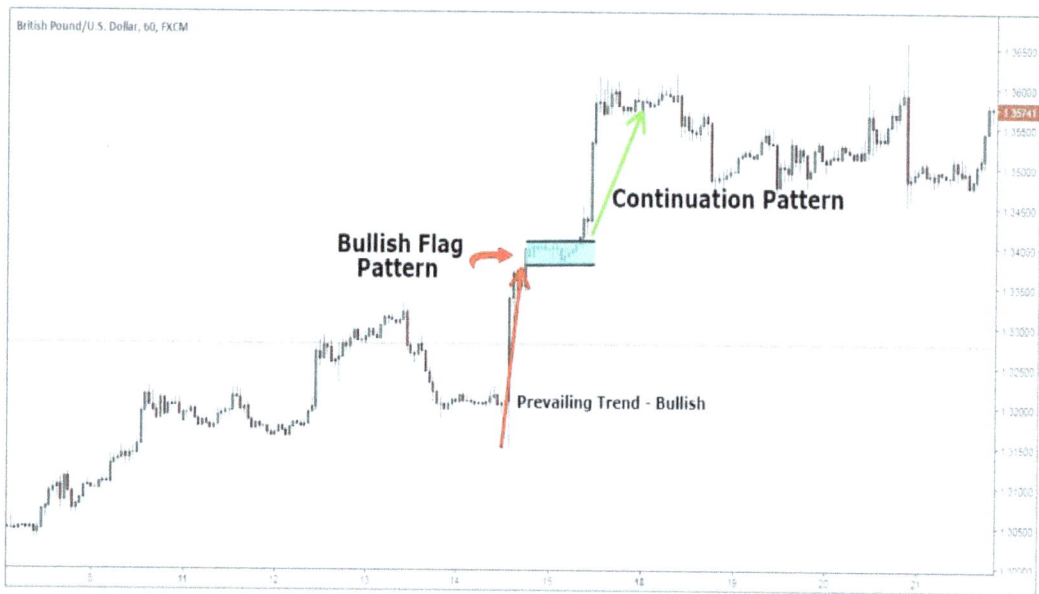

For the most part, the bullish flag pattern is a continuation pattern.

The double top pattern that is highlighted in the picture below shows an example of a reversal pattern.

It's important to find out whether the market is selling or consolidating. This is because it will show what kinds of chart patterns work best in different trade conditions. Not following this first rule is a typical reason why price action trading fails.

2. The second step is to choose the chart pattern you want to use. Do you like trading with continuation chart patterns more than reverse chart patterns? First, make sure of this!! Once you have decided on the pattern to trade, you should try to master that specific trade setup.

Repetition is the key to learning everything. Your real-time ability to spot these chart patterns will get better as you trade more of the proffered chart patterns. One of my best chart patterns is the triple top. The reason for this is the possible huge profit that could be made once a new trend starts.

3. Look for the story in the chart patterns.

Here, you need to write a story for the setups you want.

To put it simply, don't just look at the trends on the charts; look at the whole price picture. Your story needs to be in sync with your price action routine in order for it to make sense. The rest of the information needs to back that up. If you find the right way to trade, you'll win more often.

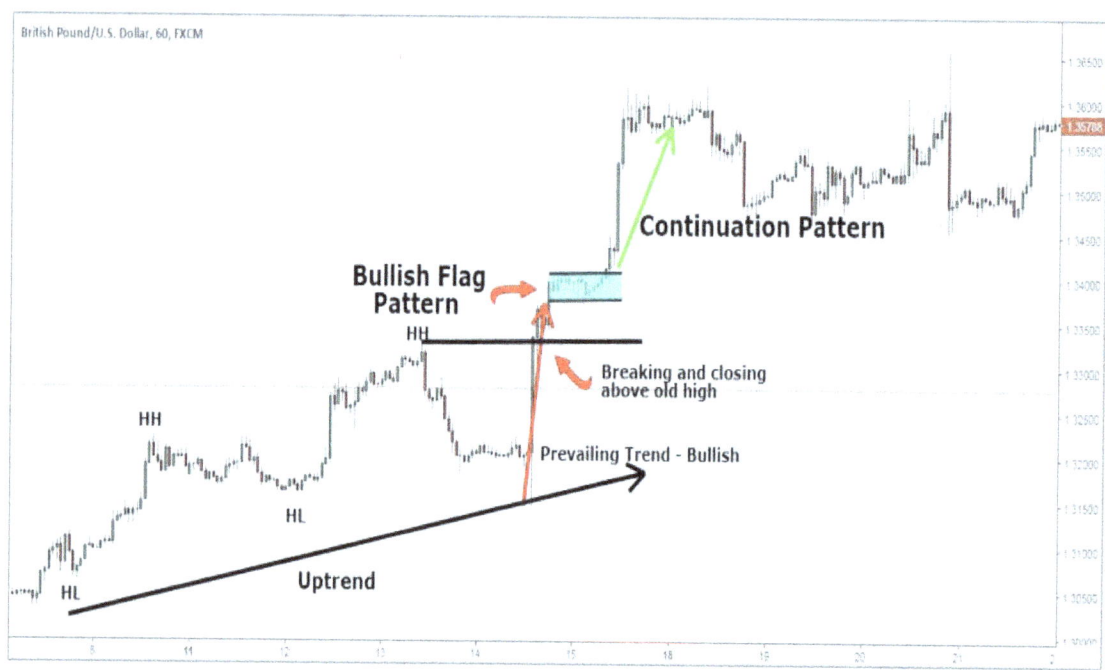

For example, it's easy to figure out what the story is behind the bullish flag that was marked in Step 1. We have had a string of higher highs and higher lows, which shows that things are going up. Second, we trade and close above a previous high, and we don't see any barriers above the market price. These are all good signs. They are strong backs for our bullish flag pattern.

4. Use a trade strategy that is based on chart patterns that meet in the right price area. (confluence)

When chart patterns are paired with good price setting, they work best. This can make our trade more confluent.

What do I really mean when I say "price area"?

To put it simply, a price area is a big place on the chart where we usually expect the price to move. The price level could be a turning point, a move high or low, or a level of support or resistance. The position may even be able to be used as a technical sign if you put them together.

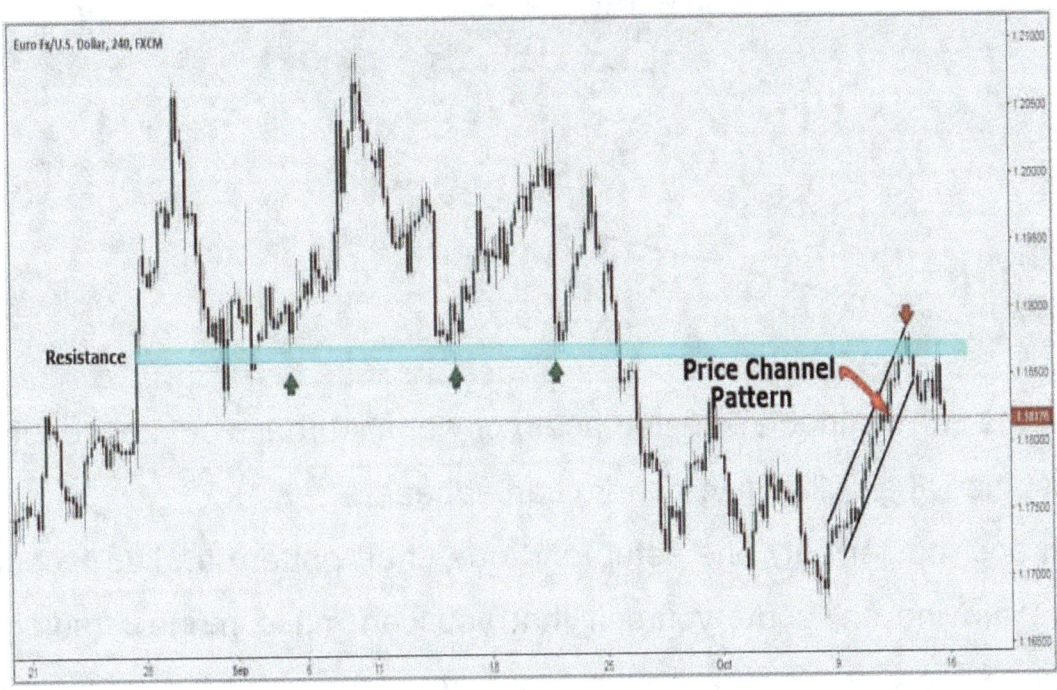

For example, the price channel pattern shown above worked because it lined up with the higher time frame's support level. The EUR/USD was going up in a range and was about to hit a point where it would stop moving up. (Resistance)

5. Make objective trading rules for trading chart patterns.

For a chart pattern trading plan to be fully developed, you need more than just a set of objective trading rules. You have to stick to your plan to the letter, but it can be changed to reflect how the market is changing. There are several ways that these chart patterns can help a trader.

A picture of this can be seen below.

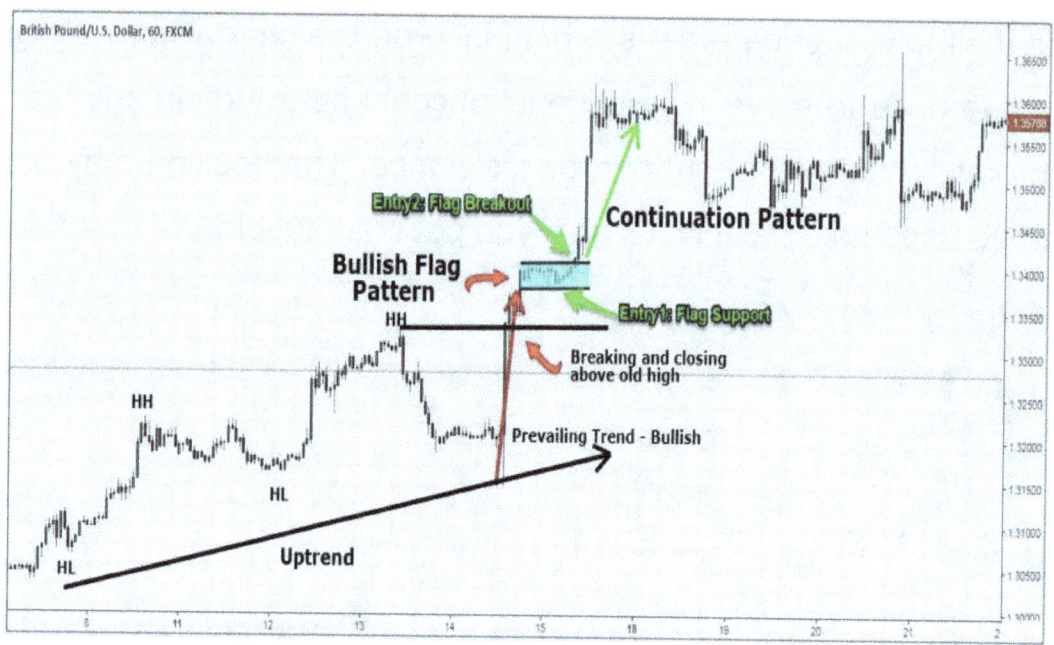

When the flag's support is tested again or when it breaks out above the flag, for instance, the bullish flag pattern can appear.

Learn and master only one setup and one chart pattern trading technique. Before moving on, show yourself that you can make money trading one pattern. Simply put, pick a pattern you like and master that chart pattern trading strategy.

CONCLUSION

Trading chart patterns doesn't have a magic bullet. You will definitely make mistakes and lose trades. The whole point is to become more selective about the chart patterns you trade.

All of the patterns talked about in this book are useful technical signs that can be used to figure out how an asset's price will move in the future and why it has moved in the past.

The reason for this is that chart patterns can show where support and resistance levels are. This can help traders decide whether to go long or short or close out open trades in case the trend changes.

Thanks a lot for reading!

- **How Many Chart Patterns Are There?**

There are many chart patterns, but they can be broken down into two groups: patterns that continue and patterns that reverse. Techs in the market use chart trends to figure out when to buy and sell.

- **Can you trust chart patterns?**

There is no doubt that chart patterns are a reliable way for traders to make accurate predictions. Some of the world's most successful traders have said that chart patterns are the reason they've been so successful over the years. Without a doubt, chart patterns do work when they are used in the right market. Price movement is the most important thing that tells you about the market and what's going on behind the scenes. If you know how to read chart patterns properly, it's easy to guess how the market will move in the future.

- **Which candlestick pattern can you trust the most?**

When it comes to candlestick pattern, the double top and double bottom stand out the most. There are a lot of different candlestick pattern. That is to say, some candlestick pattern can be trusted more than others.

- **What kind of candlestick pattern is best for bulls?**

The best bullish candlestick pattern is the bullish engulfing pattern. Bullish candlestick patterns can be used to buy stocks, commodities, cryptocurrencies, and more. Bullish candlesticks typically help identify the beginning of a new uptrend and the end of a downtrend

- **What kind of candlestick pattern is the most bearish?**

The head and shoulders pattern are the best for a bearish candlestick formation. Looking at the price chart, the Head and Shoulders shape shows that the mood has changed from bullish to bearish. According to statistics, the Head and Shoulders pattern is the most reliable way to see a trend change.